The Big City Small Kitchen *Cookbook*

The Big City Small Kitchen *Cookbook*

Cooking Without Time and Space

Anthony Michael Vitalone

Writers Club Press
New York Lincoln Shanghai

The Big City Small Kitchen Cookbook
Cooking Without Time and Space

Writers Club Press
an imprint of iUniverse, Inc.

For information address:
iUniverse
2021 Pine Lake Road, Suite 100
Lincoln, NE 68512
www.iuniverse.com

Healthy recipes for people with limited Time and Space.

ISBN: 0-595-24754-7

Printed in the United States of America

To Mom.
You have inspired my passion.
You will always guide my hands.

And

In loving remembrance of Grandma and Nana.
With a dish towel over my shoulder
And my hand rested upon my hip,
I stir in the memory of you both.

"It's all in the touch."

—Annette Marie Vitalone (Mom)

"It tastes just like candy."

—Antonio Monsanto Vitalone (Dad)

Contents

Foreword

Tony has always had an interest in cooking. Since our family is from a strong Italian background, food has always been a major 'event' during family celebrations. Tony was always involved in creating unique presentations; from appetizers to main courses to endings with fabulous desserts.

Over the years, Tony's talent has grown. Because of his extensive international travel, he has been exposed to countless cultures and their local cuisines. Our family and friends have enjoyed many meals that he created based upon what he tasted and learned while in a foreign country. He would remember which foods he enjoyed the most and, because of his gifted taste buds, could recreate and frequently change the recipe for the better. His recipes could be considered 'fusion' in nature, which is Healthy-International; centering on healthy alternatives to foods we all enjoy from around the world. There are no boundaries to the types of recipes and variations he creates. They may include flavors from China, Italy, Greece, Thailand, or Spain.

When I am entertaining and have a new idea for a certain food, I call Tony for guidelines. Quite often his suggestions will change the ingredients and also how the dish should be presented. Likewise, he will typically call me to ask for my input for a new recipe he is working on. We often discuss the pros and cons of various ingredients and of course, Tony's favorite theme, sweet versus savory.

When Tony comes home for a visit, I just turn my kitchen over to him and sit back and observe. He always brings home new techniques, food combinations and healthy alternatives. His Small Kitchen in New York City is equipped to create just about any meal from sit-down-gourmet to finger-food; a true testimony that anyone can cook regardless of the size of their kitchen.

Tony's recipes focus on tasty appetizers, homemade meals and elegant desserts. When word gets around that Tony is home for a visit the phone starts ringing. He is asked to bring a dessert for family gatherings or he will show up with an elegant appetizer. It is always a grand experience to sit down to one of his meals, because it shows his passion and desire to please the palate. If he knows someone has a favorite meal or dessert, he will out do himself to create something special for them. I guess you could say just as an artist is to his canvas, Tony is an artist in the kitchen.

I believe that if Tony chose another career, he would most definitely consider being a professional chef and perhaps he still may. As long as I can remember, he has been creating recipes for this cookbook. This collection of recipes demonstrates his talent for preparing and creating simple recipes for everyday living. If I were 20 years younger I would want to be a partner with my son in our own restaurant.

—Annette Marie Vitalone

PREFACE

My relationship with food has not always been a positive one. As a young child, I was a nightmare at the dinner table. To be honest, I do not know how I made it to age five, considering the limited number of foods I would eat. It became a showdown between me, my parents and the food, with me caught in the middle. At first, my parents were actually very patient and tried various methods of getting me to eat. My father's best attempt was to say "It tastes just like candy". Ironically, in the years to follow, my father's words would have a profound impact on my cooking style, which is strongly influence by a sweet and savory balance.

One example of my eating habits was that I would not eat red meat for various reasons. My Mom would always give me the select cut of steak in an effort to get me to eat, yet I still did not bite. As the years went on, my picky eating habits turned into stubborn defiance to the point that I would be made to sit, alone, at the kitchen table once dinner was finished until I ate my food. A great fondness and love for my sister, Joanne, was derived during this period in my life. After my parents had gone to the living room to watch television or read the obituaries, probably to see if any five year-olds had died of starvation, my sister would take a scoop of food off my plate each time she made a trip to the sink while clearing the table. To this day, she has never let me forget her merciful acts, especially on stew night. I am forever in her debt.

On one fateful night, my father had taken just about as much as he could tolerate. Even before the table was set, the battle field was in play, as it was a double whammy combination for dinner—meatloaf. Oh, the thought of red meat combined with unknown ingredients baked to a brick-life texture and served with ketchup would make me break out into a cold sweat. My Mom did her best to cut me an end piece that was well done. As I began the dissection, my father gave a stern warning to eat it otherwise, I would be wearing it. Now would be a good time to introduce you to my loving siblings; Patrick, Joanne and Vinnie. On this particular night, they found it necessary to taunt my father by saying he would never rub the meatloaf in my face. I silently agreed, after all, I was the baby of the family and I had my Mom to protect me. After years of battle I found myself on the front line, face-to-face with my Dad and the meatloaf. Needless to say, I lost that battle and there was more face-to-meatloaf than face-to-face by time dinner was over. Although the battle was lost, the war was won. As I retreated to the upstairs bathroom in an attempt to save face, I heard the final battle cry of my father that I was to cook my own food from that point henceforth. It was my liberation and set me on a journey that has lead me to numerous riches. I have never looked back and I am forever grateful to my parents for the opportunity to explore what has become one of my true life long passions.

There was one condition to the peace treaty between my parents and me. That was, if I cooked it I had to eat it; period, end of discussion. Now this was a tall order for a 10 year-old, but I accepted and never broke my word. During the first few years, I ate a lot of pasta with butter on steak nights. In addition, there were some meals I cooked, that I would have rather taken my chances with what was being served to everyone else. However, my mom stood by my side and would teach me. She would ask what I was making and would give suggestions. The times we have spent in the kitchen together are by far some of my fondest memories with my mom. I would never trade that time for anything.

Well, as fate would have it, I actually started to get it right. My mom would frequently ask to taste what I was making and finally the time came for my triumphant return. It was suggested that when I prepared some of my recipes, that I consider cooking enough for the entire family. I was more than happy to do so. All my mom had to do was ask once and I took full advantage of the request. By the time I was in seventh and eighth grades, I was making a few basic meals, but without failure I had a different dessert on the table every night. I took Jell-O to a whole new level. By the time I was in high school, I was coming home from school and starting dinner for the family. It was during these years that the early foundation recipes for this cookbook were conceived. Over the past 10 years since I have graduated from undergraduate college, I have explored my passion for food and cooking and have to my families amazement developed a sophisticated pallet. I must take a minute to say, that my mom's cooking is beyond description. The once finicky eating habits of the child in me did not appreciate the true cooking talents my mother exhibits. She claims the student has now become the teacher, however, when it comes to baking and desserts she is still the true master in the kitchen.

I hope you enjoy these recipes as much as I have enjoyed the journey which has brought me to this point. The journey has just begun. Enjoy.

Acknowledgement

Thank you to all my friends. Over the years, you have allowed me to exercise my passion. Your feedback in the final stages of this book was invaluable.

Special Thanks to Randy, Russell and Gerald.

INTRODUCTION

The Mission

I suppose living in a one bedroom apartment in New York City with a four foot by four foot kitchen has influenced my cooking over the past 10 years. When I decided to finally publish this book, I was of course looking for a theme. Several came to mind, but none of them seemed to express my true mission for having this book printed. Sometimes I am amazed at the reaction some people have to my cooking, as if they have never eating before or it is their last meal. Putting ego aside, I figured there had to be more to the story for these positive reactions.

I began to realize that many of the people I would cook for in New York did not get to eat homemade food very often. Now I am being very literal when I say homemade and not home-cooked. I consider homemade food just that—made at home, such as eggs, salt and flour to make pasta, rather than home-cooked pasta from a box. Once I realized it was the quality, freshness and unprocessed nature of my cooking that was so popular, I began to ask friends, co-workers and acquaintances one simple question; "why don't you cook?" Sounds pretty simple, but the answers I got back echoed two reoccurring themes. The first was that living in a big city makes it so easy to just walk across the street and buy a fast inexpensive meal. In addition, life in a big city is fast paced and therefore people believe they have less time to cook. Based on this feedback, I summarized the first reason why most people do not cook is a lack of Time and easy access to ready made foods.

The second reason why people did not cook was that the kitchen in their 'big city' apartment was too small or so they thought. This lack of space, in their minds, limited the equipment they could have on hand as well as simple counter area upon which to prepare foods. I summarized this reason simply as lack of Space. In the end, I came to the conclusion that for the most part, the people to whom I posed the question 'why don't you cook?', did not do so because they lived in a Big City and had a Small Kitchen. The title for this book practically wrote itself and I realized its true mission: to illustrate that healthy homemade meals are easy to prepare with limited demands on time and space.

The Essentials

Having a Small Kitchen, whether it is in a large city or small town, does not mean you should not have the equipment to cook good meals. When I was growing up I would help my father build houses, cabinets, roofs, decks or whatever a Master Craftsman is hired to do. During these years, he taught me two very important lessons when it comes to 'tools'. First, always buy the best and you will never be disappointed. These words of wisdom have applied to my life in so many ways, but probably the most in the kitchen. If you skimp and buy the $29.95 food processor, guess what is going to happen the first time you try to kneed pizza dough? Nothing. The motor will not have enough Amps to turn such a heavy mixture. So, off you will go and buy a good one that will do the job and last a lifetime. The second lesson my father taught me about carpentry, and little to his knowledge cooking as well, was to always have the right tool for the right job. As the years have passed, I have realized that this was particle to both carpentry and cooking. Not only does the right tool make the job much easier, for instance staying with the food processor example, you would not want to use a blender to dice or chop vegetables; two different tools with two different purposes. In addition to getting the job done right and fast, using the proper tool is simply safer.

Be creative when it comes to storage. I have one rule of thumb when it comes to any type of storage in my kitchen or apartment; do not "store air". That is, remove lids and stack, build shelves and simply maximize your space. The following is a list of some of the common tools in my Big City Small Kitchen. If I can get them all (plus others) to fit in my 4 x 4 foot kitchen you can too.

Cast iron skillet
Wok
Splatter Guard
Mixing Bowls
Measuring Cups
Utensil Holder
Stainless Steel Pots
Cooling Racks
Potato Ricer
Wooden Spoons
Spider Strainer
Pastry Brush
Pizza Cutter
Grease Pencil
Pastry Bag
Roasting Pans
Rolling Pin
Pasta Roller/Cutter
Food Processor
Pressure Cooker
Bunt Cake Pan
Electronic Scale

Hand-held Grater
Strainer
Sifter
Piece of Marble
Measuring Spoons
Salad Spinner
Baker's Rack
Oven Mitts
Meat Mallet
Spatulas
Potato Masher
Mellon-Baller
Salt/Pepper Mills
Vegetable Brush
Meat Thermometer
Submersion Blender
Mortar / Pestle
Culinary Set
Stand Mixer
Spring Form Pan
Microwave Oven
Cutting Boards

Deep Fry Pan
Cheese Slicer
Double Boiler
Toaster Oven
Trivets
Baking Sheets
Cookbooks
Dish Towels
Whisks
Tongs
Citrus Reamer
Can Opener
Cake Tester
Toothpicks
Pizza Stone
Mini-Fan
Loaf Pan
Griddle
Sauce Pans
Cork Screw
Blender
Pastry Shield

The Final Word

Given that the nature of this cookbook is to provide recipes that are Big City, Small Kitchen friendly, the typical serving size ranges from two to four. In the cases of soups, sauces, stews, etc. these typically will serve up to six. One of the keys to cooking in small spaces is to cook simple meals that do not require more than one or two pans. In addition, try to prepare 'starter-foods' on the weekend. These are foods you can precook and use as a base for multiple meals during the week. A few starter-foods that I always make on the weekend include, steamed rice, grilling up a few pounds of chicken breast using a simple dry rub for seasoning and preparing a fruit salad with some lemon juice (use a plastic knife and leave out the banana and sugar until ready to use). Having a few base-foods prepared in advance, will leave you with a lot of meal options for the coming week. At any given time, I typically have three to five different soups in my freezer. There is nothing better to come home to after a hectic day, than a bowl of homemade soup. Especially if it takes less than 10 minutes from freezer to table.

APPETIZERS

Black Bean Dip

This is a life saver if you are in need of a last minute appetizer.

Ingredients:

1 small onion—diced
1 tsp. olive oil
15 oz. black beans—with juice
8 oz. Salsa Sauce (see recipe)
1 cup frozen corn
1 tsp. cilantro paste (see recipe)
1.25 oz. taco seasoning
4 slices American cheese
Tortilla chips for dipping

Directions:

In a sauce pan, sauté onion and corn with oil until soft. Add beans, salsa, cilantro, taco seasoning and cheese. Simmer until smooth and begins to thicken, about three minutes. Serve warm.

Note:

The fresher the ingredients, the better this will taste. If all you have is salsa from a jar, then by all means use it. However, using fresh salsa sauce and cilantro will make a huge difference.

Variations:

You can use whatever beans you like. This can also be served as a meal. Simply serve the hot beans over white rice.

Bruschetta

This recipe is as simple as toasting bread and is a tasty appetizer.

Ingredients:

1 loaf Italian bread
6 cloves whole garlic—pealed
2 tomatoes—pulp removed—diced
¼ cup fresh basil or 1tbl. Pesto
¼ cup onion—diced
Salt and pepper to taste
¼ cup olive oil—extra virgin
Grated parmigian cheese

Directions:

Slice bread into one inch thick slices. Place on a baking sheet and toast both sides. While bread is toasting, combine tomatoes, onion, salt, pepper, olive oil and basil. Mix and set aside. Once bread is toasted, transfer from baking sheet to a cooling rack. Allow toasted bread to cool completely. Once cooled, rub garlic cloves over one side of the bread. Place bread (garlic side up) on a serving platter. Top each slice of bread with tomato mixture. Grate parmigian cheese over Bruschetta and serve.

Note:

Be sure to remove all of the seeds and pulp from the tomato. A watery tomato mixture will cause the toasted bread to become soggy.

Variations:

The toasted bread with garlic serves as a great base for endless appetizer possibilities. I will sometimes replace the tomato mixture with Hummus (see recipe).

Guacamole

This traditional dip made from fresh avocados makes a great appetizer, sandwich spread or topping for tacos.

Ingredients:

2 ripe avocados—pealed and pitted
2 cloves garlic—crushed
2 tsp. onion—diced
1 tbl. Cilantro—chopped fine
1 tbl. fresh lemon juice
¼ tsp. salt

Directions:

Place all ingredients in a non-reactive bowl (glass). Combine all ingredients by squeezing avocados through your fingers until a creamy texture is achieved. Be sure to leave some small chunks of avocado. Place one avocado pit back into the guacamole; this will help prevent it from turning brown. Serve immediately or refrigerate for up to one day in airtight container.

Note:

It is very important to allow avocados to ripen. To speed up the process, place avocados in a brown paper bag for few days. Once avocado is soft to the touch or begins to develop black spots, it is ready. If all of your avocados do not ripen at the same time, simply put the ripe avocados in the refrigerator until the others are ripe.

Variations:

If you have a very ripe tomato sitting around, this makes a great addition to guacamole. Remove all seeds and pulp and chop into small pieces. Stir in once guacamole had been hand-mixed. Additional salt may be necessary.

Hummus

While in Greece, I started to appreciate the unique and flavorful taste of hummus. It is a low fat, high fiber dip that is sure to enhance your meals.

Ingredients:

¼ cup sesame seeds
2 tbl. hot water
½ tsp. vegetable oil
3 tbl. lemon juice
3 cloves garlic
1 can garbanzo beans—retain juice
¼ tsp. salt

Directions:

Grind sesame seeds in food processor for two minutes or until rough flour texture is formed. Add hot water and oil and process until smooth. Add lemon, garlic and salt and blend until smooth. Add beans and begin to process. Begin to add a small amount of the juice from the beans to thin out the mixture. Process until smooth.

Note:

I think hummus is not only underrated, but underutilized. I like to make a batch and use it instead of mustard or mayonnaise on sandwiches.

Variations:

Most canned beans will work for this recipe. Try using black, white, or pinto beans. If you are looking for an extra healthy hummus, try using 1 ½ cup fresh soy beans that have been steamed in ¼ cup water. Additional salt is needed if using soy beans.

Puff Pastry

Once you master this pastry—the opportunities are endless. My first trip to Greece had a profound influence on my diet—a healthy one at that. This recipe is an exception, but yields the most flavorful pastry. Be sure to use very high quality butter—if you can afford it use Normandy butter from France.

Ingredients:

4 cups all purpose flour
6 ½ sticks cold unsalted butter
1 ½ tsp. salt
1 cup COLD water

Directions:

With your fingers, pinch together all ingredients. Be sure to work fast. If the butter begins to soften and melt—place in refrigerator for 10 minutes. Once all ingredients are combined, roll out on lightly floured cold marble surface with a cold marble rolling pin. Fold pastry sheet into thirds and return to refrigerator for 10-15 minutes. Remove from refrigerator, roll out and then turn into thirds again. Repeat this process six times. When you roll out for the final time, do not fold into thirds. For crescents, cut pastry into 5 inch squares. Roll into a cylinder, starting from a corner. Shape into crescent form. Place on cookie sheet, brush with melted butter and bake 375° oven for 12-15 minutes or until puffy and brown.

Note:

The result of the process of folding, chilling and rolling will yield a pastry with 18 layers. This is what causes it to puff and flake once baked. Wrap unused portion in plastic wrap and freeze. Use for any recipe which calls for puff-pastry, such as Greek Spinach Pie.

Variations:

Need a fast and tasty treat? Simply sprinkle top of pastry with cinnamon and sugar. Cut with cookie cutter or use pasty cutter to cut sheet into 2x2 inch squares. Place on baking sheet and bake 375° oven for 10-12 minutes or until puffy and brown. Remove, drizzle with Greek honey and serve.

DRINKS

Carrot Juice

This drink is very refreshing, but very filling. It is a great drink to have between meals or in the evening if the munchies hit you, since it will fill you up.

Ingredients:

3 carrots, pealed and chopped
2 ounces apple juice
3 ice cubes
1 tsp. honey (optional)

Directions:

Place juice, carrots and honey in blender. Blend on high until smooth and thick. Add ice and blend until ice is crushed. Serve immediately or keep apple/carrot mixture in an airtight container in refrigerator until ready to server. Shake well before using refrigerated mixture.

Note:

This should be served very cold.

Variations:

Go crazy with this drink. Use 6 ounces of your favorite fruit instead of the carrots such as apples, strawberries, blueberries, etc. Whatever you may have around.

Fresh Pina-Colada

As with the inspiration for a majority of my recipes, this was the result of a two-fold objective. That being, to have a fresh pina-colada that was not made from artificial flavors or sweeteners. This is always a popular drink with my friends during summer dinner parties.

Ingredients:

4 cups fresh pineapple	½ cup honey
2 cups fresh coconut	Ice cubes

Directions:
With a hammer, crack open the coconut. There are three seems that run length-wise on the coconut. Hammering on one of those seems is the easiest way to crack open the shell. Remove the meat from the shell and with a vegetable peeler, peal off the thin layer of brown membrane from the white coconut meat. Place pineapple, coconut and honey in a blender and blend until smooth. Start the blender on low and increase speed as mixture becomes smooth. This forms the pina-colada base.

To server: place 1 cup pina-colada base in a blender with 3 ice cubes for each serving. Blend on high until smooth and creamy. Serve immediately.

Note:
Only blend in ice when ready to serve. Refrigerate unused pina-colada base in an airtight container for up to three days. This is a great time saver when serving at a gathering, simply make in advance and use when ready.

Variations:
To make fruit flavored pina-coladas; add ½ cup strawberry, banana or raspberry to the base recipe.

If you prefer, add a shot of rum per serving when blending with ice.

Frozen Iced-Tea Cooler

This was one of the first iced drinks I created to help beat the heat during hot summers living in New York City.

Ingredients:

7 ice cubes (2 cups)
10 tsp. sweetened iced-tea mix
1 cup cold water
Fresh lemon-sliced

Directions:

Place all ingredients, except lemon, in blender and blend on high speed until ice is crushed. Stir in sliced lemons and serve immediately.

Note:

If you are trying to reduce the amount of sugar in your diet, use unsweetened iced-tea mix and add a few tablespoons of honey to suit your taste.

Variations:

If you are looking to have an extra special treat—try using 1 cup whole milk instead of the water.

Perfect Lemonade

Most people's idea of homemade lemonade is squeezing fresh lemons into ice water. Although that is a very refreshing drink, there are times when old-fashioned lemonade is called for.

Lemon Syrup

Ingredients:

1 part fresh squeezed lemon juice   1 part granulated sugar

Directions:

Cut lemons in half and squeeze out all juice and pulp. Typically, one lemon will yield one serving of lemonade. Remove any seeds from the juice and measure the amount of juice and pulp collected. Add the same measurement amount of sugar to the juice. For example, if you have one cup of juice, add one cup of sugar to the juice and stir. This will create the lemon syrup. You can store the lemon syrup in the refrigerator until ready to use.

To make lemonade

Ingredients:

1 part lemon syrup   3 parts cold water

Directions:

In a juice container, combine lemon syrup and cold water. For example, one cup of lemon syrup will need three cups water. Stir and serve over ice.

Note:

The key to great lemonade is fresh lemons.

Variations:

Once you combine the lemon syrup and water, you can also place it in a deep baking pan and freeze to make lemon ice. Keep stirring every 30 minutes until desired consistence is achieved.

Soy Tea (Chai)

Even if you are not a tea lover, you must give this a try. Chai is a unique method of preparing tea. Once you try this, you will not want to drink tea any other way. You may even consider switching to Chai from coffee.

Ingredients:

1/8 tsp. nutmeg
½ tsp. cinnamon
2 tsp. vanilla extract
2 cups soy milk
1/8 tsp ginger
1 tsp. pepper corns
¼ cup sugar or to taste
1 tbl. black tea leaves
1 tbl. peppermint tea leaves

Directions:

Combine all ingredients in a sauce pan and simmer 10 minutes. Pour through a fine strainer or coffee filter and serve hot.

Note:

Traditional Chai should be made with whole unprocessed spices. So, if you have cinnamon sticks, vanilla beans or fresh ginger, you will be rewarded with an even richer flavor. However, the above substitutions are just as good.

Variations:

Chai can be made with any number of combinations of teas and spices. I highly recommend you stop by a local tea merchant and pick up a few blends including black-, herbal-and spiced teas. Chinese supermarkets typically offer a great variety of unique blends. Use your imagination. Toss in any spice that you enjoy. Try anis seeds or even jalapeño pepper seeds for a kick.

You can use milk instead of soy and honey instead of sugar.

During the summer, I will make a batch and keep it in the refrigerator. Once Chai is chilled, in a blender, combine one cup of Chai liquid with one cup fat free vanilla or chocolate frozen yogurt and blend.

Tofu Fruit Shake

Give this refreshing drink a try if you are looking to cut calories. You may want to start off with the yogurt version if the jump to tofu is too big.

Ingredients:

1 cup mixed fresh fruit
1 cup apple juice
10 ounces soft (non-firm) tofu
¼ cup honey
4 cups boiling water

Directions:

In a bowl, pour boiling water over tofu and let stand for a minute. Remove tofu from water and set aside. Place fruit, apple juice and honey in a blender. Mix until smooth. Add tofu one third at a time to blender, blending between each addition. Refrigerate until cold and serve.

Note:

Uncooked tofu may contain bacteria. For this reason, it is essential that you pour boiling water over the tofu.

Variations:

Use your favorite fruits. I have found that strawberries, raspberries or blueberries work well. I do suggest always adding a banana for extra thickness.

This can also be made with plain yogurt. Replace the tofu with 8 ounces plain yogurt. You can place either the tofu or yogurt versions in the freezer for an hour to make a healthy "ice-cream".

Yogurt Fruit Shake

This drink is very refreshing and a great substitute for milk shakes. It is a fast way to us up over ripened fruits.

Ingredients:

8 ounces low fat yogurt—plain
2 cups fresh strawberries
1 tsp. sugar or honey
¼ tsp. lemon juice

Directions:

Place all ingredients in blender and mix until well blended. Refrigerate until ready to serve.

Note:

Be sure fruit is very rip.

Variations:

Substitute the strawberries for your favorite fruit. However, avoid using citrus fruits.

You can also place mixture in freezer for one to two hours, return to blender and mix until smooth before serving.

BREAKFAST

Country Home Fries

Ingredients:

2 cups potato skins
2 tbl. butter
1 tbl. paprika
¼ cup onion—diced
Salt and pepper to taste

Directions:

In a hot skillet add all ingredients. Stir well and allow to brown before stirring again. Once both sides are browned, remove from heat and sever immediately.

Note:

Whenever I need potatoes for a recipe, I always add two more potatoes than a recipe calls for. This way, when I peal them, I use a paring knife and leave a generous amount of potato with the skin. I boil the potato skins right along with the diced potatoes. Store the potato skins in an air tight container in the refrigerator until you need them. They are perfect for this recipe or use them for Potato Quiche Soufflé or Baked Potato Skins (see recipes)

Variations:

I am not a big fan of bell pepper in my home fries, but it is an option if you prefer. Avoid adding any ingredients that will release water. This will prevent the home fries from browning.

French Toast

Probably one of the all time classic comfort foods. The secret is in the quality of the vanilla extract. Be sure to buy good extract. If you happen to be in Mexico, pick up several bottles. It is much cheaper and the flavor is much more intense. I always grab several large bottles when in Mexico.

Ingredients:

2 eggs
1/3 cup milk or cream
1 tsp. cinnamon
Pinch of salt
2 tsp. vanilla
2 slices bread
1 tbl. butter
Confectioner's sugar
Sliced strawberries

Directions:

Combine eggs, milk, cinnamon, salt and vanilla. Mix well. Soak bread in egg mixture until all liquid is absorbed. Place bread on buttered electric skillet. Cook on each side only once until brown. Serve immediately with Fruit Sauce (see recipe). Top with strawberries and dust with confectioner's sugar.

Note:

Be sure the bread is totally wet before grilling. It is best to allow the toast to cook all the way through while on one side. Once cooked and the bottom is brown, flip just to brown the top.

Variations:

When I visit my parents, I make banana nut French Toast, since my dad really likes bananas. Mash one banana until it is almost liquid. Add this to the egg mixture and cook. Top with chopped walnuts and some sliced banana.

Greek Yogurt with Fresh Fruit

My first time to Mykonis, Greece, I asked a local merchant what I should eat before leaving Greece. He said grilled octopus and Greek yogurt with fruit and honey. I fell in love with both and the following recipe has become a common midday snack or dessert for me.

Ingredients:

8 ounces Greek-style yogurt—plain
2 cups mixed fresh fruit—
  bananas, grapes, kiwi, strawberries
¼ cup honey

Directions:

Cover the bottom of a serving platter with yogurt. Distribute fruit evenly over the top of the yogurt. Drizzle honey over fruit and yogurt. Serve immediately.

Note:

Greek yogurt is simply a must for this dish. It has a unique flavor and a much thicker consistency. If in a pinch and you cannot find Greek yogurt, use plain yogurt instead. However, it is well worth it to seek out the Greek-style yogurt.

Variations:

Use whatever fresh fruits you have access to. However, try to avoid using canned fruits. I find that bananas and grapes taste the best with the honey and yogurt.

Perfect Grits

There are as many ways to eat grits as there are individual grits in a bowl. This recipe is for basic grits. Add whatever other ingredients you have an appetite for.

Ingredients:

¾ cup skim milk
3 tbl. quick grits
Pinch salt

Directions:

Combine all ingredients. Microwave on full power for 3-4 minutes. Stop after each minute to stir until creamy.

Note:

I have found that using milk rather than water yields a creamier grit. Water typically evaporates before the grits are cooked, leaving the grits dry and hard.

Variations:

Some people eat their grits plain; others add shredded cheese or stir in maple syrup. My personal favorite is to stir in one mashed banana and two tbl. honey once the grits are cooked.

Potato Pancakes

Every time my mom would make mashed potatoes and there were some left over, mom would ask if she should save the mashed potatoes. Without failure, someone would say, save it for potato pancakes tomorrow. We would all laugh because no one knew how to make potato pancakes, but mom would save the mashed potatoes and they would be thrown out a few days later when discovered in the back of the refrigerator. Follow this simple recipe and you will never throw away mashed potatoes again.

Ingredients:

1 cup mashed potatoes
2 eggs
¼ cup flour
1/8 cup onion—diced
Salt and pepper to taste
2 tbl. butter
Sour cream

Directions:

In a large mixing bowl, combine eggs, onion, salt and pepper. Add potatoes and blend well until smooth. Fold in flour until there are no lumps. Add oil to a hot cast iron skillet. Drop ¼ cup of batter on skillet and flatten. Cook until brown and flip to brown other side. Top with sour cream and serve.

Note:

You can also use 1 tbl. butter and 1 tbl. oil to fry the pancakes.

Variations:

There are endless variations you can make to this recipe. One of my favorites is to add fresh scallions instead of onion and mix in ¼ cup of shredded cheese.

Potato Quiche Soufflé

I had my first potato quiche while in Spain. It had a light texture that I have never been able to reproduce; however, this soufflé version comes pretty close.

Ingredients:

5 eggs—separated
½ tsp. baking powder
2 cups potato skins—
boiled and diced
1 medium onion—chopped
2 tbl. butter
10 ounces fresh mushrooms—sliced
½ cup grated parmigian cheese
½ cup milk
1 tbl. maple syrup
Salt and pepper to taste

Directions:

Preheat oven to 425°. In a hot cast iron skillet, add 1 tablespoon butter. Sauté onions and mushrooms with salt and pepper until soft and moisture has evaporated. Meanwhile, combine egg yolks, baking powder, cheese, milk, maple syrup salt and pepper. Mix well and set aside. In a separate bowl, whisk egg whites until stiff and peaks form. Once all liquid has evaporated from mushrooms and onion, add 1 tablespoon butter and potato skins to skillet just to bring up to temperate. Once potatoes are hot, turn off heat. Fold egg whites into egg yolk mixture. Pour combined egg mixture into skillet with potatoes. Gently stir making sure egg mixture is evenly distributed and touches bottom surface of skillet. Place in oven for 15 minutes or until center is cooked when tested with a tooth pick. Remove from oven; allow to set for 10 minutes before cutting.

Note:

Be sure to cook the potatoes thoroughly before adding the egg mixture.

Variations:

If you do not have or like mushrooms, use whatever other ingredients you desire such as bell peppers, corn or diced ham.

Waffles

These waffles are as light as air. The batter is very flavorful. I simply drizzle with some maple syrup and sprinkle with powdered sugar.

Ingredients:

2 egg-separated
½ cup flour
½ tsp. baking soda
1 ½ cup sour cream
2 tbl. vanilla extract
1 ½ cup whole milk or cream
1 tbl. corn meal
2 ½ tbl. melted butter
Pinch of salt
2 tsp. sugar

Directions:

In a clean metal bowl, whip egg whites until peaks form. In a separate bowl, combine all other ingredients. Fold in egg whites. The batter will be very thin and runny. Pour ¼ cup of the batter for each waffle on a preheated waffle iron. Cook for at least 5 minutes. Do not rush this step or open the lid too soon. Allow all the steam to vent from the waffle iron. Continue to cook a few minutes after the steam has vented. It is common for the first batch to stick or burn. Simply discard this batch.

Note:

These waffles are a labor of love. The batter requires a delicate touch to combine the egg whites. The cooking process requires patience. Do not give up if the first batch sticks. Remember not to over fill the waffle iron. Allow ample cook time prior to opening. Use cooking spray before each batch to prevent sticking.

Variations:

This waffle can be served as breakfast or a dessert. Top with your favorite fruits, frozen yogurt, chocolate sauce or fruit sauces.

Yogurt Pancakes

I simply love the rich flavor that yogurt and sour cream add to baked goods. For this reason, I have replaced the milk in my pancakes with plain yogurt. If you enjoy the flavor of these pancakes, be sure to try the Waffle recipe, where I replaced half of the milk with sour cream.

Ingredients:

2 eggs
8 ounces plain yogurt
1 cup flour
2 tbl. butter—melted
1 tbl. sugar
Pinch of cinnamon
2 tsp. baking powder
¼ tsp. baking soda
½ tsp. salt
2 tbl. vanilla
1 tbl. corn meal

Directions:

Sift together all dry ingredients. Combine all wet ingredients and mix well. Fold wet ingredients into dry ingredients just until blended. Pour ¼–½ cup of batter per pan cake onto a 350° electric grill. Cook until bottom is brown before flipping. Serve with Fruit Sauce (see recipe) or maple syrup.

Note:

When it comes to making the perfect pancake, there are two very important things to remember; be sure to not over mix the batter, and allow the pancake to cook from the bottom up. Pancakes should be flipped just once.

Variations:

There is just about no limit to the different variation of flavors you can add to pancakes. To the above batter, gently fold in one cup of your favorite fruit. Strawberries, bananas, blue berries, raspberries or even semi sweet chocolate chips all work well. Avoid adding fruit that will release a lot of liquid, such as citrus or pineapple.

BREAD

Basic Pastry Dough

For the record, let me say this is my mom's recipe. This cookbook would not be complete without a good pastry dough recipe. I have tried for years to change this recipe to make it better and all attempts have failed. I came to realize it is futile to try to improve upon perfection. This dough is very versatile in its uses. It can be used for pie shells, sweet rolls or cinnamon buns to name a few.

Ingredients:

2 ½ cups flour	1 cup vegetable shortening
1 ¼ tsp. salt	1 cup ice water—with 3 ice cubes

Directions:

Place ice cubes in a one cup measuring cup and fill with water. Set aside. Sift flour and salt. Using a pastry blender, cut in the shortening until blended. Using a salad fork, gently mix in the water a little at a time. Do not mix in ice cubes. Once dough begins to come together, use your hands to gently and lightly form the dough into a ball. Do not over mix and do not knead the dough. Wrap in plastic wrap and place in refrigerator for at least an hour or until ready to use.

Note:

Unlike pasta dough that improves in texture the more you knead the dough, pastry dough is just the opposite. Once the dough comes together, stop working it. As Mom always tells me 'it's all in the touch'.

Variations:

Variations? Not in this lifetime.

Basic Pizza Dough

This basic recipe is perfect for a food processor. I use it for all my pizzas shells.

Ingredients:

1 tbl. olive oil
1 packet dry yeast
¼ cup warm water
2 tsp. sugar
½ cup warm water
2 ¾ cup flour
1 tsp. salt
Corn meal

Directions:

Combine ¼ cup water, yeast and sugar. Mix well and allow to rise five minutes. Meanwhile, put flour and salt in food processor and blend for one minute. Combine ½ cup water with oil. While processor is on, add yeast mixture. Slowly, begin to add water and oil mixture until a balls forms. If ball does not form or if dough is too dry, add more water, 1 tbl. spoon at a time until ball forms. Once ball forms, process for 30 seconds. Allow to rest in processor for two minutes, then process again for 30 seconds. Remove from processor, cover with glass bowl and allow to rise for an hour. Punch down dough after about 45 minutes and allow to rise for remainder of hour. Roll out on clean surface sprinkled with corn meal. Top with favorite pizza toppings and bake in 425° oven for 20-30 or until brown on bottom.

Note:

To make individual grilled sandwich wraps, divide dough into eight equal sections once it has risen. Roll out each section into a very thin round mini-pizza on a clean surface sprinkled with corn meal. Place on indoor or outdoor grill and grill on each side for 2-3 minutes. Fill with your favorite sandwich topping, fold like a taco and eat.

Variations:

For a healthier crust, you can also use whole wheat flour. For flavored breads, add black olives, grated cheese or diced pepperoni. Place in a loaf pan, let rise and bake.

Garlic Pizza

Ingredients:

Basic Pizza Dough (see recipe)
4 cloves garlic—crushed
½ cup pesto paste (see recipe)
10 oz canned mushrooms
2 tbl. olive oil
1/3 cup grated parmigian cheese
Salt to taste

Directions:

In a bowl combine garlic, mushrooms, oil, cheese and salt. Roll out pizza dough. Brush pesto paste evenly over the surface of pizza shell. Top with mixed ingredients. Bake at 425° oven for 20 minutes or until pizza shell is brown.

Note:

Be sure to watch the pizza as it cooks. Do not allow the garlic to burn.

Variations:

If you want, sprinkle the top of the pizza with one cup of mozzarella cheese or distribute one-tablespoon-scoops of ricotta cheese evenly over the top before baking.

No-bake Garden Pizza

Ingredients:

One recipe Basic Pizza Dough (see recipe)

One recipe Fresh Tomato Salad (see recipe)

Directions:

Prepare pizza dough as direct. However, follow the 'Note' section for grilled sandwich wraps. Top each mini-shell with Fresh Tomato Salad. Serve immediately.

Note:

Use a slotted spoon to drain off excess liquid from the tomatoes before topping the pizza.

Variations:

Try spreading a layer of Hummus (see recipe) over the pizza shells before topping with tomato salad.

Old-Fashioned (low-fat) Corn Bread

Why does corn bread have to be so fattening? After having given up corn bread for several years, due to the high butter content, I decided to create a low-fat alternative for this old-time favorite. The jalapeño peppers make up in flavor, what the lack of butter leaves behind. Traditional corn bread was cooked in a cast iron skillet. I was thrilled to resurrect this technique, as it yields a crisp crust and moist center.

Ingredients:

1 Jalapeño pepper—seeded and chopped
1 cup all purpose flour
1 cup corn meal
2 tsp. baking powder
¼ cup fresh or frozen corn
Pinch salt
1 cup skim milk
¼ cup vegetable oil
2 egg whites—beaten until foamy
1 tbl. butter

Directions:

Preheat oven to 400°. Over high heat, sauté corn with a little oil until corn is roasted and brown. Meanwhile, in a separate bowl, combine dry ingredients, and then stir in oil, milk, eggs and peppers. Remove skillet from heat and stir in butter until melted. Pour batter into skillet and distribute evenly. Place in oven and cook for 20 minutes until brown and cake tester comes out clean from the center. Remove from oven and invert on cooling rack. Cut and server hot.

Note:

Don't have a cast iron skillet, yet? (Shame on you). Simply use an 8 inch round cake pan or a deep fry pan.

Variations:

Be creative. Try substituting the jalapeño peppers with garlic.

For sweeter bread, substitute pepper with ¼ cup raisins and ¼ cup sugar.

Salad Pizza

This is my favorite way to eat pizza. The whole wheat dough makes a crisp base for the zesty salad.

Ingredients:

Whole wheat pizza dough
 (see Basic Pizza Dough)
6 cloves garlic—minced
¼ cup Pesto Paste (see recipe)
1 ½–2 cups tomato sauce
Corn meal
4 cups mixed greens
Italian Dressing

Directions:

Preheat oven to 425°. If you have a pizza stone, place it in the oven. Stretch out pizza dough on clean surface that is dusted with a little corn meal. Form a round shell that is 2 inches smaller in diameter than the pizza stone. Remove preheated pizza stone from oven and place pizza dough on stone. Using a pastry brush, brush the pesto paste over the surface of the pizza dough. Distribute tomato sauce evenly on top of the pizza. There should be at least ¼ to ½ inch of sauce on pizza dough, so be generous. Sprinkle garlic evenly over top. Place pizza back in oven. Bake for 25-30 minutes or until crust is brown. Remove pizza from oven and let cool to room temperature. Toss greens with dressing and put on top of pizza. Slice as usual and serve room temperature.

Note:

Resist the temptation to put cheese on this pizza. The garlic, generous amount of tomato sauce and seasoned greens are all you need to enjoy this pizza.

Variations:

Try using different salad dressings, however, stick with the savory varieties. A sweet dressing such as vinaigrette does not seem to blend well with the tomatoes or the garlic.

Twice Baked Pizza Primavera

The technique for this recipe was inspired by a pizza I ate while traveling through Ireland.

Ingredients:

Basic Pizza Dough (see recipe)
6 oz. black olives—sliced
½ cup onion—chopped
2 plum tomatoes—¼ inch rounds
1 clove garlic—diced
1 ½ cup ricotta cheese
8 oz. canned mushrooms-diced
2 tbl. pesto paste (see recipe)
1-2 cups tomato sauce (see recipe)
¼ cup parmesan cheese—grated
Salt and pepper to taste
¼ cup sugar
1 tbl. cinnamon

Directions:

Prepare pizza dough. While dough is rising, combine olives, mushrooms, onion, garlic and tomatoes. Season with salt and pepper, toss lightly and set aside. In a separate bowl, combine ricotta cheese with sugar and cinnamon. Once dough has risen, roll out and place on a heated pizza stone that has been dusted with corn meal. Bake at 450° for 15-20 minutes, until dough is crisp and brown on top and bottom of shell. Remove from oven. Cover bottom of cooked shell with tomato sauce. Distribute mixed vegetable evenly over shell. Using a tea spoon, distribute 'mounds' of ricotta cheese evenly over the top of the vegetables—do not smooth out ricotta. Using a spoon, dip into the pesto and drip evenly over the pizza. Top with grated parmesan cheese and bake at 450° for 5-10 minutes. Serve hot.

Note:

If the pesto is too thick, thin it out with some olive oil. Keep it in the oven the second time only until the vegetables are heated and the cheese begins to melt.

Variations:

The technique of baking your pizza shell before topping it is the point of this recipe. Once baked the first time, top it with whatever you want and bake again. This works well with toppings that just need to be heated, such as fruits, vegetables and pre-cooked meats.

PASTA

Adult Macaroni and Cheese

I loved Mac and Cheese as a child, but with most childhood favorites, this meal seems to have a stigma of being a 'kid's food'. I find alfredo sauces to be far too rich and fattening for my taste. So, I have revived this classic, with a taste more suitable for an adult's pallet and waist line. There is more depth of flavor, while reducing the amount of fat from the traditional version. Oh, and by the way, kids will like this as well.

Ingredients:

1 clove garlic—crushed
2 cups chicken stock
1 tbl. pesto paste (see recipe)
12 ounces cheese tortellini
1 tbl. butter
2 slices American cheese

Directions:

In a deep fry pan, combine chicken stock, pesto and garlic. Bring to a boil and add tortellini. Simmer over high heat until pasta is cooked and about one inch of liquid remains. Reduce heat and add cheese. Stir until melted. A creamy sauce will form. Remove from heat and stir in butter. Serve immediately.

Note:

If you do not have chicken stock, you can use 2 cups water and chicken bouillon cubes. Follow the direction on the bouillon package for the amount to use for 2 cups of water.

Variations:

This recipe is a great way to get vegetables into your diet. Toss in some mushroom or zucchini.

You can also use cheese ravioli in place of the tortellini.

Baked Lasagna

Whenever my mom would make lasagna, my brothers, sister and I would stand close at hand waiting for any scraps of torn pasta noodles, cheese and sauce. A bowl filled with all three ingredients made a great Sunday afternoon snack, which became known as 'three pot lasagna'. The following recipe is the traditional baked version.

Ingredients:

1 pound cooked lasagna noodles
3 cups Tomato Sauce (see recipe)
Grated Romano cheese
1 pound ricotta cheese
¼ cup cinnamon
3 tbl. sugar
2 eggs—raw

Directions:

Preheat oven to 350°. Combine ricotta cheese, egg, cinnamon and sugar. Mix thoroughly. If mixture is too thick, add a second egg. In a 5x9 inch baking dish, spoon a layer of tomato sauce over the bottom. Add a layer of cooked pasta, then a layer of cheese mixture. Repeat layers, starting with sauce, then pasta and then cheese until all ingredients are used. The final layer of pasta should only be topped with sauce and grated Romano cheese. Bake for 45–60 minutes. Let stand for 10 minutes prior to serving.

Note:

Be sure to put a good amount of sauce on the bottom of the baking pan, so it will not burn during baking. You can add grated cheese to each layer or just on the top.

Variations:

I have to admit; 'three pot lasagna' is still a favorite of mine as I prefer the lighter, quality of unbaked pasta. In addition, if you do not bake the lasagna, you can substitute dried pasta for fresh handmade pasta. To make 'three pot lasagna' cover the bottom of a plate with sauce, then cooked pasta noodles, some ricotta cheese and top with more sauce. Repeat several times to create multiple layers. You should omit the egg for this version.

Baked Penne

This recipe is a great shortcut when you want lasagna, but do not have much time. It is unique and a great time saver when serving a lot of people.

Ingredients:

1 pound cooked penne noodles
Grated Romano cheese
3 cups Tomato Sauce (see recipe)
1 pound ricotta cheese
¼ cup cinnamon
3 tbl. sugar
2 eggs—raw

Directions:

Preheat oven to 350°. Combine cheese, egg, cinnamon and sugar. Mix thoroughly. If mixture is too thick, as a second egg. Fold pasta into cheese mixture. Once combined, stir in half of the tomato sauce. In a 5x9 inch baking dish, spoon a layer of tomato sauce over the bottom—using half of the reserved amount. Pour pasta into baking pan and top with remainder of sauce. Cover top with grated cheese. Bake for 45 minutes to one hour. Let stand for 10 minutes prior to serving.

Note:

Be sure to put a good amount of sauce on the bottom of the baking pan, so it will not burn during cooking.

Variations:

I typically like to add some vegetables to this dish. In a fry pan, sauté some zucchini, onion and mushrooms in a little olive oil until tender or you could also sauté pealed eggplant and pitted green olives with some olive oil for an authentic Italian taste. Combine this with your pasta and cheese mixture before baking. Top with sauce as directed.

Basic Egg Pasta Dough

Ingredients:

2 eggs
1–1 ½ cup flour
Pinch salt

Directions:

Sift flour and salt. On a clean surface, make a well in the center of the flour. Place the eggs in the center of the well and begin to mix in with a fork. Once flour and eggs are combined use your hands to kneed dough until all flour is incorporated into the dough. Kneed for five minutes. Additional flour may be required if dough begins to stick. Wrap dough in plastic wrap and allow to set 10 minutes. Divide into quarters and roll out using a pasta roller. Use the linguine attachment to cut into strands. Hang over a wooden dowel to air dry 10 minutes. Place into salted boiling water and cook three to five minutes. Be sure not to over cook. When pasta is cooked, remove from water and add your favorite sauce.

Note:

If you do not have a pasta roller, you can roll the pasta by hand using a rolling pin. Be sure to flour the counter and dough well to prevent sticking. Once dough is rolled out to 1/8 inch, use a pastry cutter to cut ¼ inch wide strands. Dry and cook as described above.

Variations:

You can flavor your pasta with just about anything.

Pesto Pasta

Add one tablespoon Pesto Paste (see recipe) to the eggs and mix in as described.

Sun Dried Tomato Pasta

Combine four reconstituted sun dried tomatoes in blender with eggs. Pour into flour well and combine as described.

Spinach Pasta

Blend one cup cooked spinach with eggs in blender. Pour into flour well and combine as described.

Breaded Pasta

Try this dish when you want a fast pasta meal.

Ingredients:

1 clove garlic-crushed
1 tbl. onion-diced
1 tbl. butter
1 tbl. olive oil
Dash salt and pepper
1 cup cooked pasta
1 tbl. water—from pasta
1 tbl. seasoned bread crumbs
1 tbl. grated parmigian cheese

Directions:

Bring 2 quarts of water to a boil. Add pasta and cook until tender. In a fry pan, sauté garlic, onion, butter, oil, salt and pepper for 2 minutes. Once cooked, remove pasta from water and add to sauté pan with 1 tbl. water. Continue to cook over med-high heat until all water is evaporated. Remove pasta and vegetables from sauté pan and toss with bread crumbs and cheese. Serve immediately.

Note:

This recipe is for one serving, simply increase amount of ingredients for the number of people you are serving.

Variations:

This recipe goes well with flavored pastas, such as Spinach or Sun dried Tomato (see recipes).

Cold Sesame Noodles

This is a standard dish I take on picnics to Central Park. You can make it in advance and not have to worry about heating it up.

Ingredients:

1/3 cup Peanut Sauce (see recipe)
6 ounces uncooked pasta
2 tbl. sesame seeds
1 tbl. peanut butter
1 tsp. peanut oil

Directions:

Combine Peanut Sauce in a mixing bowl with peanut butter. Mix well and set aside. Cook pasta in salted water until tender but not over cooked. While pasta is cooking, place sesame seeds and oil in a fry pan and sauté one minute until seeds brown and begin to pop. Remove pasta from water and drain well. Combine pasta with peanut mixture and stir in sesame seeds. Refrigerate until cold before serving.

Note:

If noodles are too try or sticky when serving, add additional peanut oil.

Variations:

I typically add some chopped fresh scallions at the time of serving.

Fried Noodles with Duck Sauce

Ingredients:

Fresh Basic Pasta—see recipe
Apricot Fruit Sauce—see recipe
Peanut oil

Directions:

Make fresh pasta (see recipe) as directed, however, after rolling out, cut into two inch wide strips. Cut each strip into four inch long sections. Cover the bottom of a fry pan with one inch of oil over high heat. Once oil is hot, add the pasta to the oil. Move the noodles around so not to stick. Noodles should cook within a minute per side. Remove from oil and allow to drain on a cooling rack. Prepare fruit sauce (see recipe) with fresh apricots. Dip cooled noodles in sauce.

Note:

Watch the noodles carefully. They will actually be cooked almost as soon as they hit the hot oil. If you wait until they appear brown, you may burn them.

Variations:

I like to serve these as an appetizer when cooking stir fry. If you want, sprinkle noodles with ground ginger as soon as you remove them from the fry pan.

Garbanzo Bean and Ginger Pasta

Have you ever cooked pasta and realized you made too much once you drain off the water? If so, simply toss the extra pasta with a little olive oil and put in the refrigerator. This recipe is a great way to use up cold pasta. The key is to recognize you have made too much pasta before you add any sauce.

Ingredients:

½ fresh tomato—pealed and diced
1 carrot—pealed and chopped
3 cloves garlic—crushed
1 cup garbanzo beans
2 tbl. olive oil
1 ½ spaghetti—precooked
1 tsp. ground pepper
1 tsp. paprika
Dash of salt
1 tsp. ground ginger

Directions:

In a fry pan, sauté carrots and garlic in oil over medium heat. Season with salt, pepper and paprika. Add beans and tomato. Turn up heat and simmer for a minute. Add precooked pasta and simmer until mixed and pasta is reheated. Add ginger and mix well. Remove from heat and serve.

Note:

Do not over cook. As soon as the tomato begins to break down it is ready.

Variations:

You can use powered ginger; however, fresh ground ginger will be much more flavorful.

Garlic Lovers Pasta-Primo

This recipe has a unique East meets West flavor. One of my first roommates in New York City was Filipino. It was interesting to see that both Italian and Filipino cooking uses similar base-ingredients. This recipe is a result of trying to please both our pallets.

Ingredients:

4 tbl. olive oil
¼ cup onion—chopped
4 cloves garlic—crushed
2 dashes hot pepper sauce
2 cups broccoli—blanched and chopped
1 cup fresh mushrooms—chopped
¼ cup black olives—sliced
2 cups penne pasta—precooked
1 ½ cup Tomato Sauce (see recipe)
2 tbl. soy sauce

Directions:

In a fry pan, sauté onion and garlic in oil for about a minute over medium heat. Be sure not to burn the garlic. Turn up heat and add broccoli, olives and mushrooms. Cook just until vegetables become hot. Season with pepper and soy sauce. Add pasta and stir until well mixed. Add tomato sauce and hot sauce. Stir until pasta and vegetables are well coated. Let simmer for 2 minutes. Serve warm.

Note:

This dish will taste better if you allow it to cool slightly after cooking. If it is too hot, you will not notice the unique depth of flavors.

Variations:

Try using green olives in place of the black olives.

Glazed Pasta and Chicken

One night I was craving a flavor I remembered from my childhood. The one from that mix you would add to pasta and hamburger to help it make a great meal. This recipe will defiantly bring back memories, however without all the extra sodium and fat. If you have children, this is a must make recipe.

Ingredients:

1 large chicken breast—skinned, boned and cubed
¼ cup onion—diced
¼ cup olive oil
1 chicken bouillon cube
2 cloves garlic—crushed
½ cup uncooked pasta—Ditalini
1-2 cups water
1 tsp. butter
2 tbl. grated parmigian cheese
Pepper to taste

Directions:

Over high heat, in a fry pan or chicken fryer, sauté chicken with oil until browned and cooked. Add onion and sauté until onion caramelizes and pan begins to form a brown glaze on the bottom. Add garlic and stir for 10 seconds. Lower heat to medium and add 1 cup water, pasta and bouillon cube. Simmer until pasta is cooked and all water is evaporated. Add additional water as needed until pasta is cooked. Be sure all water has evaporated prior to adding more. There should be no liquid remaining in the pan when pasta is done. Remove from heat. Add butter and cheese and stir until blended. Serve immediately.

Note:

Remember, this is glazed pasta—there should be no liquid remaining once the pasta is cooked. The chicken and pasta will have a shinny glaze over them when cooked.

Variations:

You can use hamburger or ground chicken. However, I like the texture of the chicken chunks.

Low Salt Puntanesca

If you are like me, you have probably ordered Puntanesca from a restaurant that was far too salty. This recipe uses olive juice and pureed sun dried tomatoes, so there is little need for additional salt.

Ingredients:

1 cup fresh mushrooms—diced
1 large onion—chopped
1 cup black olives
¼ cup black olive juice
2 cups penne pasta—precooked
8 sun dried tomatoes—
  soaked in hot water
3 cloves garlic—crushed
1 tsp. dry pepper flakes
Salt and pepper to taste
Grated parmigian cheese
Seasoned croutons
½ cup olive oil

Directions:

Sauté mushrooms, onions and pepper flakes in 2 tbl. of the oil until brown and onions caramelize. While the vegetables are cooking, place sun dried tomatoes in 1 cup of water and microwave on full power for one minute. Place tomatoes and water in blender and combine until a paste is formed. Once vegetables are cooked, add olive juice to deglaze the pan. Be sure to stir well to remove all the brown stuck to the pan. Add tomato puree to fry pan and increase heat. Stir in ¼ cup extra virgin olive oil, cooked pasta and garlic. Add salt and pepper. Remove from heat and add olives and grated cheese. Server immediately.

Note:

Be sure to taste the sauce before adding any salt. The olive juice and sun dried tomato puree may be all you need.

Variations:

You can use whatever pasta you prefer. This actually goes very well with spaghetti.

Pasta and Butter Beans

This is a light pasta dish that is great during the summer.

Ingredients:

2 tbl. olive oil
1/3 cup onion—chopped
2 cloves garlic—crushed
4 cups chicken broth
2 cups dried pasta—penne
15 ounces butter beans—with juice
2 tbl. butter
1/3 cup parmigian cheese

Directions:

In a large sauce pan, sauté onion in olive oil. Add garlic and stir for one minute. Add chicken stock and bring to a boil. Add pasta and cook uncovered until pasta is cooked and almost all liquid is evaporated. Add beans and bean juice. Bring back to a boil. Remove from heat. Add butter and cheese and stir until blended. Serve immediately.

Note:

After adding beans, be sure to just bring back to a boil and not to over cook.

Variations:

You can use any 'white' style bean for this, such as cannelli or white beans. Do not use colored beans, such as black or kidney.

Pasta and Grilled Chicken

Ingredients:

¼ cup olive oil
5 cloves garlic—crushed
½ bell pepper—diced
½ cup onion—chopped
1 carrot—shredded
1 cup grilled chicken—diced
2 cups precooked penne pasta
Salt, pepper and paprika to taste
1 ½ cups chicken stock
1 tbl. corn starch

Directions:

In a fry pan, sauté garlic, pepper, onion and carrot in oil until onion becomes soft and translucent. Season with pepper and paprika (do not add any salt yet). Increase heat and add chicken. Stir in pasta and stir well. In a separate bowl, combine chicken stock with corn starch and mix well. Add to fry pan and stir until thickened. Taste and season with salt.

Note:

Be sure not to over cook once the chicken stock and corn starch mixture are added. If you do not have chicken stock, use chicken bouillon and water. Follow the directions on the bouillon container for the amount required for 1 ½ cups water.

Variations:

As with any sautéed pasta dish, add whatever vegetables you may have in the house. This is a great way to use up any leftovers.

Pasta and Peas

When I was growing up, we always knew what was for dinner when my father was cooking—pasta and peas. This recipe remains one of my all time favorite pasta dishes and comfort foods.

Ingredients:

10 ounces spaghetti
4 cups water
2 cloves garlic
2 eggs—beaten
½ cup onion—chopped
Salt and pepper to taste
1 tbl. butter
¼ cup Romano cheese
2 cups frozen peas—thawed

Directions:

Bring water to a boil; add salt, pasta, garlic and onion. Cook until pasta is tender, but not soft. While stirring rapidly, pour in the raw beaten eggs. Stir well. Remove from heat and add butter, pepper and cheese. Stir well. Serve immediately.

Note:

This recipe is best when cooked with spaghetti, rather than macaroni.

Variations:

This is a pretty low fat meal. To make it even healthier, try using whole wheat spaghetti, soy beans and egg substitute.

Pasta Natural

The 'earthy' flavors of whole wheat, spinach and soy beans combine to create a dish that is a celebration of the 'taste of nature'.

Ingredients:

2 cups chicken broth
2 cups soy beans—steamed
4 ounces whole wheat spinach pasta
Salt and pepper to taste
1 tbl. butter
¼ cup grated parmigian cheese

Directions:

In a sauté pan, bring chicken broth to a boil. Add spaghetti and bean. Simmer 5-8 minutes or until pasta is cooked. Season with salt and pepper. Remove from heat. Stir in butter and cheese. Serve immediately.

Note:

Do not cook pasta until all the liquid is evaporated; you want to have a good amount of liquid to mix with the butter and cheese.

Variations:

Try other flavors of whole wheat pasta, such as garlic or sun dried tomato.

Pasta with Chicken Sauce

Ingredients:

1 ½ cups broccoli—blanched and chopped
½ cup onion—chopped
¼ cup bell pepper—chopped
1 ½ cups penne pasta—precooked
1 tbl. olive oil
Salt, pepper and paprika to taste
1 clove garlic—crushed
1 ½ cups boiling water
1 chicken bouillon cube
1 tsp. corn starch

Directions:

In a hot fry pan, sauté broccoli, onion, pepper and garlic with oil until onions become translucent. Add precooked pasta and stir for one minute. In a separate bowl, combine water, bouillon and corn starch. Mix well until smooth. Add bouillon mixture to fry pan and cook over low heat until it begins to thicken. Taste and season as needed. Serve immediately.

Note:

If using bouillon cube rather than chicken stock, be sure to taste the sauce before adding salt. Bouillon cubes have a high salt content which may be sufficient.

Variations:

The type of vegetables and pasta you use is totally up to you. Try using asparagus rather than broccoli. In addition, if you have chicken stock on hand, simply use that instead of the water and bouillon cube.

Potato Gnocchi

Ingredients:

2 eggs
1 clove garlic—crushed
¼ cup Romano cheese
¼ tsp. salt
4 large baking potatoes
2 cups sifted flour

Directions:

Wash, peal and chop potatoes. Place in boiling unsalted water for 15–20 minutes or until fork tender. Remove and drain well. Place eggs, garlic, cheese and salt in a blender and mix well. Combine egg mixture with potatoes and hand-mash until blended, but leaving some potato chucks. On a clean surface, make a well with 1 ½ cups of the flour. Place the potato mixture in the flour well and begin to knead. Continue to knead and add additional flour until dough is not sticky. Knead for 10 minutes. Section dough in quarters. Cover the resting dough with a damp cloth until ready to use. Take one quarter of the dough and roll it out into a rope ½ inch in diameter. Cut the rope into one inch long pieces. Roll each piece of dough into a ball. Using a fork, roll the ball off the tines of the fork. Repeat for each section of the dough. Cook immediately in boiling salt water until the gnocchi float, about 3-5 minutes. Remove gnocchi from water and drain.

Note:

You can also simply wash and fork prick potatoes and place in microwave on high for 12–15 minutes. After 8 minutes, turn potatoes over. Remove and allow to cool. Slice lengthwise and peal off skins. However, this tends to dry out the potatoes, so less flour will be needed. Also, if you are in a hurry, potatoes can cook in less than five minutes in a pressure cooker. You can freeze uncooked gnocchi on a baking sheet. Once frozen, transfer to an airtight container and freeze up to three months.

Variations:

Potato gnocchi taste great with a variety of sauces. Try serving with a sauce made from pesto paste, milk and butter. If you want an even faster dish, simply toss cooked gnocchi with butter and seasoned breadcrumbs.

Ravioli with Wine Sauce

This is a fast meal that will satisfy any pasta craving.

Ingredients:

6 cheese ravioli
3 cloves garlic—crushed
6 tbl. olive oil
1 onion—chopped
5 fresh mushrooms—sliced
Salt and pepper to taste
½ cup white wine
1 tsp. butter
Grated parmigian cheese

Directions:

Boil ravioli in salted water for 5-10 minutes or until they float. Do not over cook. Remove from water and set aside. In a skillet over high heat, sauté garlic, onion and mushrooms in olive oil. Season with salt and pepper and cook for about 2 minutes. Reduce heat and add wine, allow to simmer for a few minutes until alcohol is evaporated. Add ravioli to skillet. Turn up heat and sauté for 2 minutes. Remove from heat and stir in butter. Serve immediately. Top with grated cheese.

Note:

If you are using homemade ravioli, be sure not to over cook in the water. If using frozen ravioli, be sure to not cook them all the way in the water. They will continue to cook in the wine sauce and will absorb more flavors.

Variations:

You can use any type of dried pasta for this recipe. However, since the cheese from the ravioli adds to the flavor, you may want to add ½ cup cream to the sauce or serve the pasta over a thin layer of ricotta cheese.

RICE

Fried Rice

Ingredients:

2 carrots—shredded
½ cup corn
½ cup peas or soy beans
1 cup cooked chicken—diced
2 tbl. peanut oil
1 tsp. sesame oil
2 cloves garlic
½ tsp. ground ginger
2 cups precooked white rice—cold
2 tbl. soy sauce
2 raw eggs—scrambled
½ cup onion—diced
1 tbl. water

Directions:

In a very hot wok, add eggs and water. Using spatula, scramble eggs until cooked. Remove egg and set aside. Allow wok to become very hot again. Add both oils along with carrots, corn, peas and chicken. Stir fry for one minute. Add rice, ginger and soy sauce. Continue to stir fry over very high heat until rice does not stick to wok. Add onion, garlic and cooked eggs and stir for one minute. Remove and serve immediately.

Note:

It is important to use cold rice. Be sure to make rice the night before and refrigerate. See Perfect Rice recipe.

Variations:

The great thing about fried rice is that you can put pretty much anything in it. This is a great way to use up left over vegetables or grilled meats.

Perfect Rice

Rice is a major part of my diet. However, I am sensitive to the aluminum taste that often occurs when using an automatic rice cooker. Follow this basic recipe and not only will you have perfect rice every time, but never have to endure that aluminum taste again.

Ingredients:

1 part long grain white rice 2 parts water

Directions:

Place rice in sauce pan and rinse thoroughly in hot water. I typically rinse it 10 times. Drain well. Add water, stir and bring to a boil. Stir several times while rice is coming to a boil. Once water boils, stir one last time and reduce heat to a low simmer. Cover and let it simmer 10 minutes. Do not open the lip and do not stir it again. When no more steam is venting or you begin to hear a sizzling, remove the lid and gently tip the pan to see if any water remains. If so, do not stir, recover and allow to cook until water is gone. When no water remains, remove from heat and let it set for a few minutes uncovered. Fluff with a fork and serve.

Note:

The rule to remember, always use twice as much liquid by volume as rice. By not stirring during the cooking process, air vents are created that allow the water to evaporate and 'steam' the rice. If you stir during cooking, these vents are not created and water cannot evaporate, leaving you with a sticky mess.

Variations:

You can use chicken stock in place of water. Also, try sautéing a bunch of your favorite vegetables such as mushrooms, onions, garlic and zucchini and add them to the washed rice when you add your water or chicken stock. Cook using the same directions. See Winter Rice recipe for an example.

Rice and Beans

Ingredients:

2 cups cooked rice—
see Perfect Rice recipe
1 medium onion—chopped
15 ounces canned black beans—
with juice
2 cloves garlic—crushed
1 cup frozen corn
1 tbl. fresh cilantro—minced
2 tbl. olive oil
2 slices American cheese
1 cup frozen soy beans
2 tbl. Salsa Sauce (see recipe)
2 tbl. taco powder

Directions:

In a fry pan, sauté onion with oil until tender, but not soft. Stir in garlic, beans with juice, corn and soy beans. Lower heat and add salsa, cilantro, taco power and cheese. Stir until cheese melts. Remove from heat and serve over cooked rice.

Note:

This is a fast recipe. If you cook the rice at the same time, both rice and beans should be done in less than 10 minutes.

Variations:

Add whatever vegetables you have around, however, the beans are a must. You can also use pinto, kidney or white beans.

Risotto Verdi

If you enjoy risotto, try this recipe. I reduced the butter and serve the cheese on the side, so each person can control how much is added.

Ingredients:

1 medium onion—diced
2 tbl. butter
2 tbl. olive oil
1 clove garlic—diced
8 oz. mushrooms—diced
Grated Romano cheese
½ cup frozen spinach
¼ cup fresh basil—diced
1 cup Risotto—uncooked
3 cups chicken stock
Salt and pepper to taste

Directions:

In a deep sauté pan (chicken fryer if you have one), combine all ingredients except chicken stock. Sauté for a few minutes until mushrooms begin to brown and rice is coated with oil and butter. Over medium heat begin to add chicken stock one cup at a time. Stir continuously until all liquid is absorbed before adding each additional cup of stock. When you add the third cup, lower the heat and taste for seasoning. Cook away enough of the final cup of stock until risotto is creamy, but not dry or stick. On a dinner plate, distribute ½ inch thick of risotto evenly over plate surface. Serve immediately.

Note:

Leftover risotto is a no-no. This is a dish best served when first cooked. However, if you make too much, refrigerate until ready to eat. To reheat, add risotto to a sauté pan and add just enough chicken stock to moisten. Do not over cook; just bring the risotto back to temperature.

Variations:

You have unlimited options when it comes to risotto. The 'base' for risotto is oil, butter, risotto and chicken stock in the proportions listed above. Beyond the basic four ingredients, you can create any variation. If you are looking for a traditional southern Italian risotto, add the juice and zest of two lemons along with ¼ cup diced mint leaves. Season with salt and pepper to taste.

Shrimp and Garlic Fried Rice

Ingredients:

1 onion—diced
1 carrot—shredded
2 raw eggs—whisked
½ pound fresh shrimp—
  shelled and de-veined
5 cloves garlic—crushed
¼ cup soy sauce
1 tsp. sesame oil
1 tbl. peanut oil
1 tsp. ground ginger
¼ cup onion—diced

Directions:

In a hot wok, scramble-cook eggs. Remove and set aside. Bring the wok's temperature back up and stir fry garlic and carrots in both oils for 30 seconds; be sure not to burn the garlic. Add shrimp and ginger and cook until pink. Add rice, eggs and soy sauce. Continue to stir until blended and rice begins to brown. About a minute before removing from the heat, stir in the diced onion. Server immediately.

Note:

Be sure rice is cold. Make it the night before and refrigerate.

Variations:

You can use any meat for this recipe such as chicken or beef.

Winter Rice

This is a great way to add flavor to what would normally be plain rice. Serve as a side or main dish.

Ingredients:

¼ cup olive oil
½ medium onion—diced
4 fresh mushrooms
15 ounces canned white beans—with juice
1 cup zucchini—diced
1 chicken bouillon cube
1/2 cup water
½ cup uncooked long grain rice

Directions:

Over medium-high heat, sauté onion with oil until onion is brown and begins to caramelize. Add mushrooms and cook one more minute. Add rice and stir constantly for two minutes. Add additional oil if sticking to the pan. Once a brown glaze is formed on the bottom of pan, add water, bouillon cube, zucchini and beans with juice. Allow to come to a boil, stirring often. Once liquid begins to boil, stir one last time, reduce heat and allow to cook covered for 10 minutes.

Note:

If you recall from the Perfect Rice recipe, you always want 1 part rice to 2 parts liquid. Since the juice from the beans is added to this recipe, you only need ½ cup water.

Variations:

You can significantly change the overall flavor of this simply by adding a few cloves of fresh garlic and some pesto paste.

CHICKEN

Chicken Cacciatore

This is a fast and healthy version of an Italian classic.

Ingredients:

1 ½ pounds chicken breast—skinned, boned and cubed
1 medium onion—chopped
2 cups zucchini—chopped
1 bell pepper—seeded and chopped
1 clove garlic—crushed
10 ounces fresh mushrooms—halved and sliced
¼ cup olive oil
5 cups Tomato Sauce (see recipe)
2 tbl. pesto paste (see recipe)
Salt and pepper to taste

Directions:

Clean and prepare chicken. Season with salt and pepper and set aside. In a preheated skillet or chicken fryer, sauté chicken and oil until browned on the outside. While chicken is browning, cut vegetables. Once chicken is cooked, transfer to a separate clean bowl. In the same skillet (using the same oil the chicken was cooked in), add the onion, zucchini, bell pepper and mushrooms. Season with salt and pepper and cook on high heat until vegetables begin to soften. Add garlic, pesto, chicken and tomato sauce. Lower heat and simmer for 30 minutes to allow favors to blend. Serve over a bed of rice or cooked pasta.

Note:

Be sure not to over cook the chicken or vegetables, as they will still cook during the final 30 minutes of simmering.

Variations:

I prefer to serve this over a bed of plain rice or with some pasta. If you are looking for lasagna that is over the top, use this cacciatore sauce in place of tomato sauce for lasagna.

Low Fat Chicken Salad

There are a few reasons why I would never eat chicken salad; celery, mayonnaise and the chance of chicken gristle. This is my solution to all three. The over powering celery has simply been omitted, fat-free yogurt replaces the mayonnaise and as with all my chicken recipes, only the leanest fat-free chicken is used. I originally used hummus to replace the mayonnaise; however, my mom recommended the yogurt, which works perfectly.

Ingredients:

2 lbs. chicken breast—grilled and diced
2 strips turkey bacon—cooked and diced
2 scallions—chopped
4 hard boiled eggs—chopped
One granny smith apple—diced
8 oz. fat-free Greek yogurt
2 cups corn—grilled
½ cup golden raisins
Salt and pepper to taste

Directions:

Combine all ingredients and mix well. Refrigerate and serve.

Note:

Taking the time to grill the chicken and corn really compliments the smoky flavor of the turkey bacon. To grill the corn, simply place fresh or frozen corn in a skillet with some peanut oil and sauté until brown.

Variations:

For a change, I will grill up some shrimp in place of the chicken. Also, if you are really trying to cut calories, you can remove the egg yolks.

Low fat Orange Chicken

If you are looking for a light meal that is low in fat, try this one out.

Ingredients:

2 pounds chicken breast—skinned and boned
4 cloves garlic—crushed
1 cup orange juice
¼ tsp ground ginger
Rind of one orange-grated
2 tsp. spicy mustard
Salt and pepper to taste

Directions:

Preheat oven to 350°. Fillet and slice chicken breast into eight pieces and place in a roasting pan. Place all other ingredients in a blender and mix until smooth. Pour marinade over chicken and bake for 34 minutes to one hour. Serve over steamed rice. Spoon liquid over chicken and rice. Top with slices of fresh orange.

Note:

Be sure to keep watching the chicken. Since this is low in fat, the chicken could dry out if cooked too long.

Variations:

Once chicken is done cooking, remove chicken from roasting pan and set aside. Place roasting pan over low heat and thicken with 1 cup corn starch/milk mixture. Remove from heat and stir in 2 tbl. butter. Serve as directed.

Spicy Chicken and Green Beans

This is a great meal to make the day after a picnic or BBQ. It is fast and no one will recognize it may have come from leftovers.

Ingredients:

4 tbl. olive oil
1 pound grilled chicken breast—precooked and diced
1 cup fresh green beans—chopped
Pinch of salt
1 tbl. fresh ground pepper
2 tbl. soy sauce
1 ½ cups precooked rice
3 cloves garlic—crushed

Directions:

Sauté garlic with oil in fry pan for one minute. Stir in chicken and beans. Season with salt, pepper and soy sauce. Add rice and stir well. Remove from heat as soon as chicken and rice are hot, since they are precooked, it will not take more than a few minutes.

Note:

This recipe gets its heat from the pepper; feel free to add even more if you like fresh ground pepper.

Variations:

This recipe works well with just about any leftover grilled meats. If you do not have beans, then use fresh corn or peas.

Fish

Baked Fish

This light marinade is perfect for allowing the flavor of your favorite fish to come through.

Ingredients:

2 tbl. butter—melted
1 tbl. fresh lemon juice
2 cloves garlic—crushed
1 tbl. onion—grated
Salt and pepper to taste
4 dashes liquid pepper sauce
1 tbl. peanut oil
1 salmon fillet—1 inch thick

Directions:

Preheat oven to 475°. Combine all ingredients except fish and oil. Mix well and set aside. In a very hot cast iron fry pan, sear fish fillet in oil on each side for one minute. Remove from heat and cover fillet with mixed butter sauce. Place in oven for five minutes. Remove from oven and serve immediately.

Note:

This marinade can be used when grilling fish, such as shrimp or scallops.

Variations:

You can use any type of fish fillet you prefer. Just be sure it is at least 1 inch thick. Baking time may need to be increased or decreased depending on thicker or thinner fillets.

Salmon Cakes

Try this recipe for a unique variation on Crab Cakes.

Ingredients:

2 cups potato—quartered and boiled in salt water
1 pound fresh salmon—skinned, boned and cut into 'dice-size' pieces
2 tsp. wasabi paste
2 cups seasoned bread crumbs
1 tbl. onion—grated
½ cup corn meal
¼ tsp. salt
¼ tsp. pepper
2 cups olive oil—for frying
3 eggs

Directions:

Place boiled potatoes in a large mixing bowl. Add wasabi paste, eggs, onion, salt and pepper. Mix well until smooth. Add salmon and corn meal and fold in gently. Begin to heat oil in a cast iron skillet. Meanwhile, pour bread crumbs in a separate baking pan. Form salmon mixture into patties (1 inch thick by 3 inches in diameter) and gently press into bread crumbs until well coated. The mixture will be pretty soft and sticky but will hold together once breaded. Place breaded cakes on a baking sheet. Once all cakes are breaded, begin to set into skillet. Fry on each side until browned. The cakes will brown and cook very fast; within four minutes per side. Remove to paper towel to drain off excess oil. Serve hot with Corn and Papaya Chutney (see recipe).

Note:

Be sure to gently place the cakes into the hot oil. Try using a metal spatula to slide them into the oil.

Variations:

When it comes to fish cakes, use your imagination. Although I prefer crab or Salmon, you can use your favorite fish. Just be sure to remove all bones and skin. If you do not have wasabi paste, you can use an equal amount of fresh garlic, horseradish or even fresh ginger.

Shrimp Scampi

I am not sure, but I think this was one of the first meals I ever cooked for my family. It is a fast and simple way to prepare shrimp.

Ingredients:

8 tbl. butter
4 tbl. olive oil
1 pound fresh shrimp-shelled and de-veined
Juice of one fresh lemon
1 cup white wine
1 tbl. fresh parsley—diced
3 cloves garlic—crushed
Grated parmigian cheese
Steamed white rice (see recipe)

Directions:

Sauté garlic in a fry pan with butter and oil. Add lemon juice, wine and parsley. Allow to simmer for five minutes. Turn up heat and add shrimp. Sauté shrimp for two minutes or until shrimp is pink. Do not over cook. Remove from heat and top with cheese. Serve over rice.

Note:

If you want to intensify the flavor of your scampi, wash and reserve the shrimp shells. Add cleaned shells with lemon juice, wine and parsley. Simmer for five minutes and remove shells. Turn up heat and follow recipe as directed.

Variations:

I am always looking for ways to add vegetables to my diet. Try adding some julienne carrot sticks at the same time you add the shrimp. They add color, flavor and texture.

FRUITS

Perfect Papaya

While visiting my friend Fr. Tony in the Philippines, I was introduced to and learned to appreciate tropical fruits. He reviled to me the key to maximizing the flavor of a papaya. In my opinion, papaya with lime is simply the most refreshing of all fruits or all foods for that matter.

Ingredients:

4 cups fresh papaya—cut into cubes
1 fresh lime—juiced

Directions:

Combine papaya with lime juice and gently mix. Place in an air tight container and refrigerate one hour.

Note:

The longer the papaya and lime are allowed to blend, the better the flavor. Making this 24 hours in advance is recommended.

Variations:

If the papaya is fresh and ripe, there is no need to add anything else. However, in the off season, if the papaya is not sweet enough, add 1 tablespoon honey.

Rainbow Fruit Salad

This is a unique fruit salad since it is so colorful and uses unusual fruit combinations. Rather than sweetening with sugar, I prefer to use lemon and honey in all my fruit salads. Both compliment the variety of flavors in this salad.

Ingredients:

1 cup fresh strawberries—sliced
1 cup fresh papaya—chopped
1 fresh mango—chopped
1 cup fresh honeydew—chopped
1 cup fresh blue berries
1 cup red grapes—halved
Juice of half a fresh lemon
¼ cup honey

Directions:

Combine all ingredients. Mix well and allow to set a few hours. Serve cold.

Note:

If you ever decide to put bananas in your fruit salad, be sure to cut then with a plastic knife and soak in equal amounts of lemon juice, water and a little honey. Do not add them to the salad until just before serving. This will prevent the bananas from browning and softening. If serving this or any food to infants, reserve a portion before adding the honey. Honey contains bacteria that can be harmful to infants.

Variations:

Use your imagination. Whenever I make a fruit salad, I pick a word and select my fruits from the letters in the word. For example, 'BOAR' fruit salad would have Bananas, Oranges, Apples and Raisins. The above recipe was a result of matching the colors of the fruits to the colors in the rainbow and has become a favorite of mine.

Yellows and Oranges

Fruits and vegetables that are orange and yellow are high in vitamins and antioxidants. This recipe is a tasty way to get your daily supply.

Ingredients:

2 carrots—shredded
2 oranges—supremed
1 mango—diced
1/2 cup yellow raisins

Dressing

4 tsp. vegetable oil
1 tbl. sugar
1 tbl. vinegar
1/4 tsp. salt
Dash black pepper
2 dashes red pepper sauce

Directions:

Combine carrots, oranges, mango and raisins and set aside. In a glass jar, combine all dressing ingredients and shake well. Add enough dressing to coat the carrot mixture. Serve as a summer salad or dessert.

Note:

If serving as a dessert, drizzle 1 tablespoon honey over the top before serving.

Variations:

You can also use fresh cantaloupe or papaya in place of the mango.

VEGGIES

Baked Potato Skins

Ingredients:

2 cups potato skins—boiled
2 tbl. olive oil
Dash cayenne pepper
Salt and pepper to taste

Directions:

Pre heat oven to 425°. Combine all ingredients in a mixing bowl. Toss with your fingers until potato skins are well coated. Pour out onto a non stick baking sheet in a single layer. Place in oven for 10—15 minutes or until potato skins are brown and crisp. Remove from oven and add additional salt if desired.

Note:

Whenever I need potatoes for a recipe, I always add two more potatoes than a recipe calls for. This way, when I peal them, I use a paring knife and leave a generous amount of potato with the skin. I boil the potato skins right along with the diced potatoes. Store the potato skins in an air tight container in the refrigerator until you need them. They are perfect for this recipe or use them for Potato Quiche Soufflé or Country Home Fries (see recipes)

Variations:

The sky is the limit when it comes to different seasonings. Try using garlic powder or curry powder for a unique taste.

Breaded Broccoli

Ingredients:

1 head fresh broccoli	2 tbl. olive oil
¼ cup seasoned bread crumbs	Parmigian cheese-grated

Directions:

Wash broccoli and remove all leaves. Using a paring knife, peal off outer layer from broccoli stalks. Blanch entire broccoli head and stalk for 2 minutes in boiling water. Remove, drain and put in cold water. Cut broccoli into quarters, length wise. Place broccoli quarters side by side on a baking sheet covered with aluminum foil. Pour bread crumbs over the top of broccoli. Drizzle with oil and top with grated cheese. Place under broiler for five minutes or until cheese is melted and begins to turn brown. Remove and serve immediately.

Note:

If you have a toaster oven, this works best, since you can easily see if the broccoli is ready. If you use an oven broiler, keep door cracked open and check often.

Variations:

Try substituting broccoli with cauliflower or asparagus.

Corn and Papaya Chutney

This is a great topping for anything grilled, especially fish.

Ingredients:

2 cups fresh or frozen corn
1 cup papaya—diced
1 tsp. peanut oil
Salt and pepper to taste
Juice of half a lime

Directions:

Over high heat, sauté corn with oil, salt and pepper until corn begins to brown. Add papaya and lemon juice. Cook one additional minute. Serve on top of grilled fish or Salmon Cakes (see recipe).

Note:

Be sure to allow the corn to brown. It will result in a sweet flavor.

Variations:

Try using mango and lemon juice in place of the papaya and lime juice.

Mashed Potatoes

Ingredients:

5 baking potatoes—pealed chopped and boiled
Salt and pepper to taste
1–2 tbl. butter
1–1 ½ cups hot milk

Directions:

Boil potatoes in salted water until fork tender, drain water from pot. Leaving potatoes in the same pot, add butter, milk, salt and pepper. Mash by hand until smooth, but leaving a few pea-sized lumps. Serve immediately.

Note:

You can also cook potatoes in a microwave oven if you are short on time. However, potatoes will be much drier, so additional milk will be required. However, when time is short, reach for your pressure cooker. It only takes about five minutes to cook potatoes this way.

Variations:

Garlic Mashed Potatoes

Add 1-2 crushed cloves garlic to potatoes while mashing.

Banana Mashed Potatoes

Use white potatoes, egg-corn squash or sweet potatoes.
Add one ripened banana and ¼ cup brown sugar while mashing potatoes.

Nutmeg Mashed Potatoes

This tastes great during the holidays.
Use white potatoes, egg-corn squash or sweet potatoes.
Add 2 tbl. nutmeg and ¼ cup brown sugar to potatoes while mashing.

Perfect Baked Potatoes

Follow this simple recipe and you will never have to eat a baked potato that is pasty and starchy again.

Ingredients:

1 Idaho whole potato—washed
1 tbl. olive oil
Salt to taste

Directions:

Pre heat oven to 425°. Using a fork, prick the potato several times. Coat unpeeled potato with oil and season with salt. Place right on rack of oven. Bake for 45 minutes or until potato does not resist when pricked with a fork. Remove from oven and serve immediately.

Note:

It is essential that you prick the potato with a fork. This will create vent holes for moisture to escape. Trapped moisture will cause the potato to be 'gummy'. For this reason, it is important to not wrap the potato in foil. This will only hold the moisture in.

Variations:

This is a tried and true technique for a perfect baked potato. I never bake my potatoes any other way.

Roasted Veggie Chili

With such a variety of flavors, you will never miss the meat.

Ingredients:

Group A

1 large onion—chopped
2 jalapeño peppers—halved and seeds removed
5 cloves garlic—cut in half
1 bell pepper—cut into 8ths
1-2 tbl. oil

Group B

2 zucchini—cubed
8 oz. mushrooms—chopped
2 cups frozen corn—thawed
2 tbl. chili powder

Group C

2 tsp. cilantro—diced
2 28 oz. canned tomatoes—pureed
2 15 oz. can kidney beans—with juice
2 tsp. Worcestershire sauce
1 tsp. pepper
1/8 tsp. cayenne pepper
½ tsp. salt
2 tbl. chili powder

Directions:

Combine Group A and toss well. Spread out on a baking sheet in a single layer and slow roast in a 400° oven until vegetables are soft and begin to brown. While vegetables are roasting, in a hot cast iron skillet, sauté Group B ingredients until 'toasted' and brown. Remove vegetables from oven and dice. Combine all Group A and Group B ingredients in a large sauce pan. While cast iron skillet is still hot, add ¼ cup water to deglaze; add deglazed liquid to sauce pan. Over high heat, add Group C ingredients to sauce pan and bring to a simmer. Allow to simmer for 20—30 minutes, stirring often. Serve.

Note:

This chili tastes better the next day or after it has been frozen.

Variations:

This chili can be served alone or with any starchy food. Some suggestions: pasta, rice, garlic bread or even couscous.

Spinach Italiano

Once I took advantage of a sale on fresh spinach, however, I purchased far too much. In two days, I realized the spinach was going to spoil before I could eat it all. Cooked spinach has less volume than fresh, so what was a large quantity cooks down very well. If you are ever faced with fresh spinach that is about to spoil, this recipe is a tasty solution.

Ingredients:

1 lb. fresh spinach-washed
¼ cup extra virgin olive oil
1 tbl. butter
2 cloves garlic—crushed
¼–½ cup seasoned bread crumbs
1 tsp. lemon juice

Directions:

In a large sauté pan, heat oil and butter until melted. Stir in garlic and then add spinach. Sauté until spinach begins to wilt. Just prior to removing from heat, toss with bread crumbs and lemon juice. Serve hot.

Note:

Cook the spinach for as long as you wish. I prefer to cook the spinach long enough until the leaves are dark and wilted, but the stems are still firm.

Variations:

If you are looking for a richer taste, try making creamed spinach. Rather than adding the bread crumbs, use 1 cup cream and omit the lemon juice. Top with your favorite grated cheese.

Vegetarian Meatballs

I began to make my meatballs with ground chicken but they were always too dry. As a result, I started to add vegetables to provide moisture. My recipe eventually evolved to a point where it was mainly vegetables, so I just omitted the chicken.

Ingredients:

Group A

2 cloves garlic—crushed	2 cups zucchini—diced
1 small onion—diced	5 fresh mushrooms—diced
1 carrot—shredded	1 tbl. butter
2 tbl. olive oil	Pinch salt

Group B

1 Egg	1/3 cup Romano Cheese—grated
1 ½ cups seasoned bread crumbs	Pepper and paprika to taste

Directions:

Preheat oven to 350°. Combine 'Group A' ingredients in a fry pan and sauté with butter and oil. Cook vegetables until soft. Combine 'Group B' ingredients in a separate bowl. Remove vegetables from heat, add to egg mixture and mix well. Slightly mash the mixture so to resemble a meatball texture. Form balls by rolling 2 tbl. of mixture in the palm of your hand. Place on a non-stick cookie sheet and bake for 20-30 minutes. Serve with Fresh Marinara Sauce (see recipe).

Note:

Add 1 tbl. water (or Marinara Sauce if already prepared) as needed to ensure sauté does not burn while cooking. Unused veggie-balls can be frozen and reheated under a broiler.

Variations:

Veggie-balls can be fried as well. In a fry pan, heat 1 inch of olive oil. Place veggie-balls in the hot oil and brown. Turn to brown all sides.

SALADS

Caesar Salad

By the time the raw egg scare came about in the early 90's, I was already hooked on Caesar salad. My sister Joanne and I decided one night that the egg was not all that important. To make up for the egg, we quadrupled the amount of garlic—a fair trade off. The following recipe is a result of our efforts. Do not be afraid of the garlic.

Ingredients:

1/3 cup extra virgin olive oil	Pinch of salt
4 cloves garlic	Fresh ground pepper to taste
2 dashes Worcestershire sauce	¼ cup grated parmigian cheese
2 tsp. lemon juice	Fresh Romaine lettuce or Spinach

Directions:

Place all ingredients (except lettuce) in a blender and puree until well blended. Toss with romaine lettuce. Serve immediately.

Note:

It is best to use fresh lemon juice. Bottled juice tends to create a bitter taste.

Variations:

You can cut back on the garlic if it is too strong for you. If you want to use an egg, use a coddled egg. Place an egg (still in its shell) in salted boiling water for 1-2 minutes. Remove from the shell and add to blender.

Dessert Salad

I was raised to eat my salad at the end of a meal. Over the years, my salad would typically serve as my dessert. This sweet salad can serve as your leafy greens while satisfying your sweet tooth for dessert.

Ingredients:

6 cups mixed greens
2 large strawberries-sliced
15 seedless grapes—halved
1 tbl. honey

Directions:

Combine all ingredients just prior to serving. Toss lightly and serve immediately.

Note:

For best results, be sure greens and fruit are dry and cold.

Variations:

Use your favorite fruits. I have even used mixed fruit salad before. For an added treat, I enjoy tossing in a few dried dates that have been diced.

Fresh Tomato Salad

When I think of my father's garden and my mother's cooking at the same time, Fresh Tomato Salad comes to mind. All of my grandparents had past on before I was old enough to cook for them, however, I do have a fond memory of running out to the garden to make this salad for my mother's father. This salad is a must during the summer when tomatoes and basil are in season.

Ingredients:

2 fresh tomatoes—sliced
1 clove garlic—crushed
1 tbl. onion—chopped
¼ cup fresh basil or 1 tbl. pesto
¼ cup olive oil
Salt and pepper to taste

Directions:

Combine all ingredients and allow to marinate until juicy. Serve room temperature with a generous slice of Italian bread.

Note:

This is a summer salad and requires the ripest tomatoes. If you make this during the off season, be sure to purchase vine ripened tomatoes or allow them to ripen in your window sill for a few days.

Variations:

If you have them, toss in 1/8 tsp. diced fresh hot peppers.

Grape and Nut Salad

This is a refreshing salad anytime of the year. The sugar glazed nuts and grapes compliment the raspberry dressing.

Ingredients:

¼ cup shelled walnuts—halved
1 tbl. granulated sugar
2 tbl. Raspberry Vinaigrette (see recipe)
½ cup seedless red grapes—halved
1 tsp. water
2 cups mixed greens

Directions:

In a sauté pan, cover the bottom with sugar and sprinkle water evenly over the top. Cook over med-high heat until sugar melts. Add walnuts and stir constantly until well coated and sugar begins to turn brown. Remove from heat and transfer walnuts to a sheet of aluminum foil to cool. Wash and dry greens. Combine greens, grapes and nuts. Toss with dressing. Serve immediately.

Note:

Be sure the sugar has fully melted and caramelized over the nuts before removing from the heat. If you remove them too soon, there may be sugar crystals on the outside of the nuts.

Variations:

Strawberries go well with this as well.

Meatless Taco Salad

Giving up red meat did not mean I was going to give up one of my favorite foods—tacos. This recipe is easy to make and packed with flavor. It takes less than 10 minutes to make and even less time to clean up.

Ingredients:

Group A

1 tsp. peanut oil
2 cups cooked rice—cold
¼ cup onion—diced
2 tbl. soy sauce
1 tbl. taco powder

Group B

1 cup tortilla chips—broken up
2 slices American cheese
¼ cup fresh tomatoes—diced
1 cup lettuce—shredded
2 tbl. Guacamole (see recipe)
1 tbl. Salsa Sauce (see recipe)

Directions:

Sauté Group A ingredients in a hot fry pan until rice begins to brown and stick to pan. Place Group B ingredients in a large mixing bowl. Once cooked, add cooked rice to Group B and toss. Serve warm.

Note:

Be sure to scrape and use any browned rice that sticks to the bottom of the pan. As hard as it may seem to believe, this crisp rice actually tastes a lot like the skin on a Thanksgiving turkey.

Variations:

The seasoned rice can also be used for tacos or in sandwich wraps.

Santa-Fe Salad

This is a fast salad to make and tastes best when served at room temperature. You can also serve it as a dip with baked tortilla chips.

Ingredients:

1 ripe tomato—seeded and diced
12 ounces frozen or fresh corn—removed from cob
1 cup fresh cilantro—diced
Vegetable oil
¼ cup scallion—chopped
15 ounces black beans—drained
Salt and pepper to taste

Directions:

Combine all ingredients and allow to set a few hours before eating.

Note:

Fresh ingredients are a must for this recipe. If you have vine ripened tomatoes and fresh corn on the cob even better.

Variations:

If you have a few extra minutes, I prefer to sauté the corn in a hot cast iron skillet until the corn begins to brown. Remove from skillet and follow recipe as directed.

Tabouleh Salad

Living in New York City and vacationing in Greece have greatly influenced my diet. The following salad takes just minutes to prepare and is one of my favorites. It makes a light and healthy salad or snack.

Ingredients:

½ cup couscous
½ cup hot water
2 scallions—diced
1 large ripe tomato—diced
5 oz. black olives—diced
Juice of one lemon
Zest of one lemon
¼ cup fresh parsley—chopped fine
Salt and pepper to taste

Directions:

In a mixing bowl, combine couscous with water. Stir and set aside for five minutes. Meanwhile, prepare all other ingredients. Once couscous has absorbed all the water, fluff with a fork and combine with all ingredients. Mix well and serve.

Note:

Most couscous recipes indicate cooking the couscous in boiling water for a few minutes. I have never had success with this method, as the couscous seems to cook too fast and becomes gummy. I have found that the best way to cook couscous is to simply pour hot water right from the tap over the couscous and set aside until the water is absorbed. Be sure to always fluff the couscous with a fork.

Variations:

The above recipe includes the traditional Tabouleh ingredients (except olives and lemon zest, which are my additions). However, I typically make Tabouleh when I have lots of vegetables I need to use up. As long as you include couscous, parsley and lemon juice which are the foundation for Tabouleh, you can add whatever you desire and still call it Tabouleh. However, only use fresh uncooked vegetables.

DRESSINGS

Creamy Tomato Spread

Use this as a low-fat alternative to mayonnaise on sandwiches.

Ingredients:

½ cup fresh tomato
2 tbl. pesto paste (see recipe)
1 tbl. olive oil
1 tbl. onion
1/8 tsp. salt

Directions:

Place all ingredients in blender and combine until smooth and creamy.

Note:

Be sure to blend this well so the tomato skins are well blended.

Variations:

If the tomatoes have a lot of pulp the mixture may become too juicy. Simply remove the pulp from one or both tomatoes before blending to make a thicker sandwich spread.

Honey Balsamic Vinaigrette

I created this vinaigrette because I wanted a fast salad dressing that would go with either sweet or savory salads.

Ingredients:

3 tsp. balsamic vinegar
6 tsp. honey
Pinch of salt and pepper

Directions:

Combine all ingredients in a mixing bowl and whisk well. Toss with mixed greens and serve.

Note:

This dressing is best when made fresh, rather than refrigerated.

Variations:

If you want a sweet salad, toss with fresh spinach and sliced strawberries. For a more savory salad, try tossing with mixed greens and top with shaved parmigian cheese. Since the flavors of the honey and balsamic vinegar blend well; toss with mixed fresh fruits for a refreshing appetizer.

Raspberry Vinaigrette

Clearly, I am a big sweet and savory fan when it comes to my cooking. I had always tried to appreciate the flavor of commercial raspberry vinaigrette, however, store bought versions were always too high in vinegar. I figure, if you are going to put raspberry dressing on your salad, it should taste like raspberry. This recipe is easy to make and has just enough acidity to offset the tart taste of raspberry.

Ingredients:

½ cup fresh or frozen raspberries—thawed
1/8 cup vinegar
¼ cup apple juice
2 tsp. vegetable oil
2 tsp. honey
Pinch of salt

Directions:

Place all ingredients in blender and blend until smooth. Serve over mixed greens.

Note:

This dressing holds its emulsification, however, depending on the type of fruit juice you use, it may separate during refrigeration. Simply give it a good shake before using. Dressing should be used within a few days of making.

Variations:

I like to have fun with this recipe. To be honest, I simply grab whatever fruit juice is in the refrigerator. Try using orange juice, pineapple juice or cranberry juice instead of the apple juice. My typical way of serving this dressing is over fresh spinach with sliced strawberries.

Tomato Salad Dressing

When I was growing up, during the summer, my mom would make a fresh garden tomato salad that was simply delicious. My sister, who did not like to eat vegetables, would only want the juice from the salad so she could dip Italian bread in it. After making my mom's tomato salad a few years ago, I was left with a lot of left over juice once the salad was eaten. I recalled my sister's preference for the juice and thought it was a waist to discard. I tasted the juice and figured if I could make an emulsification; it would make a great salad dressing.

Ingredients:

½ cup fresh tomato pulp—
from two tomatoes
¼ cup fresh basil or 1 tbl. pesto
or ½ tsp. dried basil flakes
2 cloves garlic—crushed
Salt and pepper to taste
¼ cup olive oil

Directions:

Put all ingredients in a blender and blend until creamy. Refrigerate at least one hour.

Note:

This is a perfect dressing after making Brochette (see recipe), since the pulp is removed in the brochette recipe.

Variations:

Some grated parmesan cheese can be added, but not too much otherwise the dressing will become too thick.

MARINADES

All Purpose Marinade

This is one of my standard marinades. It has great depth of flavor and works well for both indoor and outdoor grilling.

Ingredients:

1 egg
1/3 cup soy sauce
½ tsp. sesame oil
¼ tsp. ground ginger
Pepper to taste
8 drops liquid smoke
5 dashes hot pepper sauce
2 tbl. peanut oil
2 cloves garlic—crushed

Directions:

Place all ingredients in a blender and mix on high until foamy. Pour marinade over two pounds skinless chicken breast and let stand for at least 30 minutes. Lightly dredge chicken in flour seasoned with salt and pepper. Cover the bottom of a cast iron skillet with ½ inch peanut oil. Cook chicken on both sides until brown. Serve warm.

Note:

Be sure to allow chicken to brown before turning. A light crust will form on the outside from the flour. If you turn it too soon, the crust will break off.

Variations:

This marinade is great for grilled chicken as well. Simply marinate chicken as directed, but do not dredge chicken in seasoned flour before grilling. Baste chicken with marinade while grilling.

Basic Sweet and Savory Dry Rub

If you need a fast seasoning for meat, fish or poultry—keep this dry rub in mind.

Ingredients:

1 tsp. salt
1 tbl. fresh ground pepper
1 tsp. cayenne pepper
¼ cup brown sugar

Directions:

Grind all ingredients with a mortar and pestle. Rub on outside of meat or fish and grill.

Note:

Be sure to lower the heat on the grill, since the sugar may burn before the meat is cooked.

Variations:

If you have sea salt, this is a perfect recipe to use it.

Cilantro Paste

I needed to buy cilantro every time I wanted to make Guacamole or Salsa Sauce (see recipes). However, I simply hated to buy a whole bunch and see so much go to waist, since I would only need a small amount. One day while making basil-pesto, I looked over at a bunch of cilantro and said why not make cilantro-paste and freeze it for later. I have not thrown away unused cilantro since then. Having cilantro on hand has greatly improved the taste of my Mexican recipes.

Ingredients:

2 cups fresh cilantro leaves—packed tightly
1 tbl. olive oil
500 mg. Vitamin C-crushed

Directions:

Remove cilantro leaves from their steams and wash thoroughly in cold water. Allow to dry completely. Place cilantro in food processor and pulse until volume is reduced by half. Add oil and blend until smooth. Freeze in ice-cube trays overnight. Pop out once frozen and refreeze in an airtight container.

Note:

I have a few 'special' ice cube trays that I only use for freezing pesto/cilantro/parsley pastes. Fill trays with cilantro paste and freeze overnight until frozen. Pop cilantro cubes out of tray and place in an air tight container. I typically wrap the cubes in plastic wrap to help prevent freezer burn. Return to freezer. Each pesto cube is about 1 tbl. spoon.

The vitamin C is optional; however, it will keep the cilantro looking green and vibrant, rather than turning dark or black once thawed.

Variations:

This paste is to be used for seasoning any Mexican dish.

Dry Rubbed Pork Chops

Ingredients:

1 tsp. salt
1 tbl. fresh ground pepper
1 tbl. garlic powder
1 tbl. dried basil
1 tsp. cayenne pepper
2 cloves garlic—sliced
1 carrot—diced
1 stalk celery—diced
1 small onion—chopped
2 pork chops—1-2 inches thick
1 cup fresh mushrooms—chopped
4 tbl. butter
2 cups white wine
1 cup milk
1 tbl. corn starch
Garlic Mashed Potatoes (see recipe)

Directions:

Preheat oven to 325°. Grind salt, pepper, garlic powder, basil and cayenne pepper with a pestle. Set aside. Trim fat from pork chops. Rub pork chops with mixed seasonings on all sides. Place pork chops in a hot cast iron skillet with oil. Brown on each side for three minutes. Remove from heat and add carrots, celery, onion, mushrooms, 2 tbl. butter and sliced garlic to the pan. Place in oven and cook for 45 minutes for each pound of pork. Cook until internal temperature is between 160°—170°. Remove from oven and transfer pork to a separate covered dish to rest. Return fry pan to stove over low heat. Deglaze pan with white wine. Cook until liquid is reduced by half. Combine milk with corn starch and add to wine sauce. Stir until sauce thickens. Remove sauce from heat and stir in remaining 2 tbl. butter. Place pork chops on a bed of garlic mashed potatoes and spoon wine sauce over the top.

Note:

Be sure to taste sauce once it thickens. Add additional salt if necessary.

Variations:

If you prefer, use two butter-fly steaks. However, use red wine instead.

Paprika Marinade

There is no question, that this is my favorite marinade. I simply love the flavor of the paprika.

Ingredients:

1/8 cup vinegar
¼ cup peanut oil
1 egg
1 tsp. salt
2 tsp. pepper
1 tbl. paprika
4 dashes liquid smoke
4 dashes hot pepper sauce

Directions:

Place all ingredients in a blender and mix on high until creamy. Pour over 2 pounds skinless chicken breast and allow to marinate for at least 30 minutes. Cook over high heat on an indoor or outdoor grill. Baste with marinate while grilling.

Note:

If you do not have a bottle of liquid smoke, be sure to pick one up the next time you are at the store. The flavor of this recipe is greatly based upon the liquid smoke.

Variations:

This marinade can be use for pork as well. If you have access to an outdoor grill, I recommend you use that. However, an indoor grill is sufficient.

Pesto Paste

There is no reason to wait until the summer to enjoy the taste of basil. Peso is a must-have item in my freezer. It is easy to make and lasts for months. The uses for it are endless.

Ingredients:

4 cups fresh basil leaves—packed tightly
1,000 mg. vitamin C supplement-crushed
¼ cup raw almonds—chopped
5 cloves garlic—pealed
¼ cup olive oil—extra virgin

Directions:

Remove basil leaves from their steams and wash thoroughly in cold water. Allow to dry completely. Place basil leaves in food processor and pulse until volume is reduced by half. Add garlic, almonds and vitamin C. Process until all is well chopped. Add olive oil and process on high until smooth. Use a spatula to push mixture down a few times while processing. Use immediately or freeze for up to six months.

Note:

I have a few 'special' ice cube trays that I only use for freezing pesto/cilantro/parsley paste. Fill trays with pesto paste and freeze overnight until frozen. Pop pesto cubes out of tray and place in an air tight container. I typically wrap the cubes in plastic wrap to help prevent freezer burn. Return to freezer. Each pesto cube is about 1 tbl. spoon.

The vitamin C is optional; however, it will keep the pesto looking green and vibrant, rather than turning dark or black once thawed.

Variations:

If you are going to use this as a sauce for pasta, simply add salt, pepper and grated parmigian cheese to taste. Milk can be added to make a cream sauce.

Roasted Garlic Spread

This is a great way to prepare garlic when you want the flavor, but not the strong garlic smell. Use it to flavor just about any dish or simply spread it on toast or your favorite sandwich.

Ingredients:

1 bulb fresh garlic
3 tsp. olive oil
1/8 tsp. salt

Directions:

Preheat oven to 350°. Slice the top off the garlic bulb to expose a small amount of the garlic. Do not peal or break garlic bulb apart. Rub the bulb with 1 teaspoon oil and place root side down with cut side up. Place in oven and bake for 30 to 40 minutes until garlic begins to brown and is soft when pinched with tongs. Remove from oven and allow to cool until you are able to handle with your bare hands. Squeeze soft garlic out of each section. Place garlic, 2 teaspoons oil and salt in a mortar. Using a pestle, mash until smooth.

Note:

Be sure to allow the garlic to cook fully before removing from oven. This will ensure a smooth texture.

Variations:

You can add this to Mashed Potatoes, Fresh Pasta Dough, Salmon Cakes or even Corn Bread (see recipes) for a rich garlic taste.

SAUCES

Fresh Cranberry Sauce

I simply love Thanksgiving dinner and cranberry is one of my favorite fruits. However, canned cranberry sauce always had a metallic flavor and seemed too smooth to me. Not to mention it is always served in the shape of the can it came in. One Thanksgiving, my parents came to spend the holiday with me in New York City. The following is the cranberry sauce I served and it has been a part of our family's Thanksgiving dinner ever since. My originally recipe called for oranges; however the cranberries made them taste a bit flat. My mom promptly recommended pineapple—we have not changed it since then.

Ingredients:

1 granny smith apple, pealed, cored and diced
10 oz. canned pineapple—diced
12 oz. fresh cranberries
1 cup water
1 cup sugar
¼ cup walnuts—chopped

Directions:

Bring water and sugar to a boil. Add cranberries and bring back to a boil. Lower heat and simmer for 10 minutes, stirring often. In a large mixing bowl, combine apples, walnuts, and pineapple. Pour hot cranberry mixture over apple mixture and stir. Refrigerate before serving.

Note:

The longer this recipe sits the better it tastes. My mom and I would fight over the leftovers three days after Thanksgiving. If you can find fresh cranberries, this is a very refreshing dessert anytime of the year.

Variations:

For an extra tangy sauce, use pineapple juice in place of the water. Add additional water if there is not enough pineapple juice to equal one cup.

Fresh Marinara Sauce

This is a fast and light sauce to serve over fresh pasta.

Ingredients:

1 onion—diced
2 cloves garlic—crushed
2 cups canned tomatoes—crushed
1 tbl. olive oil
¼ cup Romano cheese—grated
¼ cup fresh basil—torn
Salt and pepper to taste

Directions:

In a sauce pan, sauté onion with olive oil until translucent. Add garlic, basil, tomatoes, salt, pepper and cheese. Simmer for 10 minutes. Serve.

Note:

If you want to reduce the garlic flavor, add it to the onions a minute before adding the remaining ingredients. Be sure not to burn the garlic. If the sauce begins to thicken too rapidly, lower heat and add a little water to thin out.

Variations:

If you do not have fresh basil, you can use 2 tbl. pesto or 1 tsp. dried basil flakes.

Fruit Sauce

This sauce goes perfect with cakes, French Toast (see recipe) or ice-cream.

Ingredients:

1 cup fresh fruit—strawberries or blueberries or raspberries
¼ cup confectioner's sugar
2 tsp. lemon juice
Pinch of salt

Directions:

Place all ingredients in a deep container and blend with a submersion blender until smooth. If using raspberries and you do not want any seeds, push sauce through a mesh strainer. Refrigerate until ready to use.

Note:

A hand held submersion blender works best. However, a standard blender can be used.

Variations:

Use pretty much any non-citrus fruits you desire. If using fruits other than those listed above, you may need to adjust the amount of sugar depending on the sweetness other fruits have.

This recipe works well with frozen fruits as well. It can be used as a topping or eating alone. Follow directions, however, use frozen fruit. You may want to place fruit in microwave on full power for 20 seconds just to soften slightly.

Hot Fudge Sauce

Have you ever had a craving for a Hot Fudge Sunday, but had no hot fudge in the house? Follow this simple recipe and enjoy a fast and tasty chocolate sauce, which is lower in fat than store bought hot fudge.

Ingredients:

6 ounces semi-sweet chocolate chips
¼ cup coffee liquor
½ tsp. cinnamon
¼ cup skim milk
1 tbl. butter

Directions:

Melt chocolate chips with liquor in double boiler. When melted, stir in cinnamon. Remove from heat, add butter and milk. Stir until butter is melted. Server immediately over frozen yogurt. Store unused portion in airtight container in refrigerator. Microwave to reheat.

Note:

Be sure not to get any water in the chocolate while in the double boiler.

Variations:

The coffee liquor and cinnamon add a nice depth of flavor; however both can be omitted if serving to children. Try using a dash of flavored extracts, such as orange or your favorite liquor, such as amoretto.

Peanut Sauce (for Satay)

This is my version of a traditional Thai Satay sauce. It tastes great over anything grilled, such as chicken, tofu, octopus, or vegetables.

Ingredients:

2 scallions—chopped
3 cloves garlic—crushed
4 dashes hot pepper sauce
2 tsp. honey
1 tbl. vinegar
2 tbl. light soy sauce
2 ½ tbl. crunchy peanut butter
½ tsp. lemon juice

Directions:

Combine all ingredients and mix well. Allow to set a few minutes before serving. Use as a dipping sauce for grilled foods.

Note:

Not using light soy sauce may cause the sauce to be salty.

Variations:

You can vary the amount of peanut butter to make a thicker or thinner sauce. If you have extra sauce, do not throw it away. Simply use this sauce to marinate chicken or pork before cooking. I have even thinned out this sauce with peanut oil and used it as a unique salad dressing.

Salsa Sauce

I began my quest for a homemade salsa upon growing tired of all the sugars added to store-bought salsa. I stumbled upon a small Mexican restaurant in New York City that had the best fresh salsa I had ever tasted. I offered to buy the recipe, but it was not for sale. So, I bought half a gallon instead and proceeded to examine it with a magnifying glass; roasted vegetables was the secrete. I am grateful for my efforts, as the restaurant has since closed.

Ingredients:

½ cup fresh cilantro—packed
¼ cup onion-chopped
2 jalapeno peppers—with seeds
3 fresh tomatoes—cored
½ tsp. sugar
1 tsp. salt—to taste
1-2 cloves garlic
2 tsp. vinegar
Vegetable oil

Directions:

Cut peppers and tomatoes in half and coat skin-sides with oil. Place peppers and tomatoes on a baking sheet cut sides down. Broil on top rack of oven for 20-30 minutes or until pepper and tomato skins are blackened. Remove from broiler and place peppers and tomatoes with their blackened skins, juices and seeds in food processor with all other ingredients. Pulse just a few times until blended, but not too much. Be sure to leave some chunks. Refrigerate.

Note:

The heat of the salsa can be adjusted by the amount of jalapeno seeds you use. I like my salsa on the hot side, so I leave all the seeds in. However, I have found that the seeds of one jalapeno are enough to add just the right amount of heat for most people.

Variations:

If you want a thicker salsa, add one tablespoon tomato paste, however, I have found that once the salsa sets overnight it thickens up.

Spinach and Pesto Sauce

This sauce combines two of my favorite flavors. This sauce is pretty low in fat and high in flavor. It is a fast and unique alternative to tomato sauce.

Ingredients:

1 cup wilted spinach
1 tbl. pesto (See Recipe)
2 slices American cheese
½ cup reduced fat milk
1 small onion—diced
Olive oil
2 cloves garlic—crushed
Salt and pepper to taste
¼ cup parmigian cheese—grated
1 tbl. butter
2 servings cooked pasta

Directions:

Sauté onions with oil until translucent. While onions are cooking, place spinach, milk and pesto in a blender and puree until smooth. Add spinach mixture to onion once cooked. Stir in cheeses. Simmer five minutes. Add garlic, butter, salt and pepper just before mixing into pasta. Sauté pasta with sauce for one minute. Serve immediately.

Note:

Add additional milk at anytime while cooking if sauce becomes too thick.

Variations:

Fresh or frozen spinach can be used. If using fresh spinach, wilt it in a fry pan with a little water. If using frozen, defrost in microwave. This sauce tastes great in Risotto (see recipe), as well. Simply add some to the Risotto once the final amount of liquid has been absorbed by the Risotto during cooking.

Tomato Sauce (Gravy)

As a young boy, I pretty much grew up holding my mom's apron strings in the kitchen. I think I have watched my mom make her tomato sauce several hundred times. This is my version of my mom's unmatchable tomato sauce.

Ingredients:

2 large onions—diced
1/3 cup extra virgin olive oil
4 cloves garlic—crushed
56 oz. tomato puree
36 oz. tomato paste
56 oz. water
2 tsp. salt
1 tbl. fresh ground pepper
2 tbl. pesto
4 tsp. sugar
6 oz. Romano cheese—grated
2 tbl. garlic powder
1 tsp. dried basil

Directions:

In a sauce pan, sauté oil and onion over low heat until onion is completely translucent and begins to caramelize. Do not rush this; allow to cook for at least 15 minutes without onions turning brown. Add garlic and stir of one minute. Add tomato puree and water. Increase heat, cover pan and simmer for 30 minutes. Add tomato paste and stir in completely. Add remaining ingredients and still until blended. Simmer on very low heat for at least one hour. Refrigerate until ready to serve.

Note:

This sauce is ready to use after cooking, however, I have found that freezing the sauce first creates a richer flavor.

Variations:

If you are looking for a deeper flavor to your sauce, you can cook meatballs, chicken or sausage in the sauce over low heat for a few hours.

Vegetable Sauce

If you are looking to fill up on your daily vegetables, this is a great sauce.

Ingredients:

3 tbl. olive oil
1 clove garlic—crushed
½ medium onion—diced
1 head broccoli—diced
1 ½ cups frozen spinach—thawed
1 cup canned tomatoes—crushed
¼ cup water
¼ cup Romano cheese—grated
Salt, pepper and paprika to taste
Gnocchi, penne or pizza shell

Directions:

Sauté onion and garlic over medium heat for one minute. Add broccoli and sauté for one minute more. Turn up heat; add spinach, tomatoes, water, cheese, salt, pepper and paprika. Bring back to a simmer and allow to simmer over high heat for 1 to 2 minutes to allow any extra water to cook off. Fold in cooked pasta and continue to cook for another one minute.

Note:

At anytime during cooking, additional olive oil may be used if vegetables begin to stick to the pan.

Variations:

This sauce is a great topping for pizza as well. Be sure to cook longer so the sauce is thick before using on pizza.

SOUPS

Chicken Broth

This makes a light broth that is great for cooking pasta, rice or potatoes. Use it in place of water for any soup recipe.

Ingredients:

1 tbl. olive oil
1 cup carrots—chopped
2 cups chicken trimmings—uncooked
1 stalk celery-chopped
2 cloves garlic—crushed with peel
1 onion—chopped with peal
8 cups water
Salt and pepper to taste

Directions:

In a sauce pan, sauté all ingredients expect water until they begin to brown. Add water and bring to a boil. Lower heat and simmer for 30 minutes. Remove vegetables and chicken parts from broth. Strain broth through a coffee filter. Store in refrigerator or freeze in air tight plastic container.

Note:

I make chicken stock on the weekends from any vegetables in the crisper from the previous week. I typically grill a few pound of chicken breast for the coming week and this is a great way to get use out of the chicken bones, skin and fat trimmings.

Variations:

You can add just about any uncooked vegetable to this recipe. I have found that including a few leaves of fresh spinach adds great flavor and color.

Low-fat Broccoli Soup

This basic recipe is very low in fat and full of flavors. I typically will serve this over a bed of rice or toasted garlic bread that has been chopped into large cubes.

Ingredients:

Chicken bouillon cubes
(enough for 6 cups water)
8 cups water
2 carrots—chopped
1 stalk celery—chopped
1 large onion—chopped
4 heads and stalks broccoli
5 ounces mushrooms-chopped
½ tsp. black pepper
½ tsp. salt
1/8 tsp. cayenne pepper
1/8 tsp. ground nutmeg

Directions:

In a large pot, bring water to a boil. Meanwhile, in a separate fry pan, sauté carrots, celery, onion and mushrooms until soft and begin to brown. Remove flowerets from the broccoli stalks. Rinse flowerets and dip into boiling water for one minute. Remove from water and set aside. Using a paring knife, remove the outer fibrous layer of the broccoli stalks and then chop. Add bouillon cubes to the same water you blanched the broccoli flowerets in. Add chopped broccoli stalks and cooked vegetables to the water/bouillon mixture and bring to a boil. Chop broccoli flowerets and add to soup once it is boiling. Season with salt, pepper, cayenne and nutmeg. Remove from heat immediately. Using a submersion blender, blend until smooth.

Note:

An upright blender can be used instead of a submersion blender, however, be sure to blend the soup a small portion at a time, so not to overflow the blender. Hot liquids expand when blended.

Variations:

If you want to indulge, you can add either one cup heavy cream or 2 tbl. butter or grated parmesan cheese or even some sour cream.

Mom's Chicken Soup

Whenever someone in my family had a cold, Mom would make her chicken soup without failure. Even today, I turn to chicken soup to recover from a cold; however, it seems to work best when Mom makes it.

Ingredients:

1 large onion—chopped
2 cups celery with leaves—chopped
2-3 cups carrot—diced
3 lbs. fresh whole chicken—with skin and bones
2 48 oz. cans chicken broth
3 cups water
2 tsp. salt
1 ½ tbl. pepper
1 head fresh escarole—washed and quartered bottom 3 inches cut off

Directions:

Combine all ingredients except for escarole in a large pot and bring to a boil. Once boiling point is reached, reduce heat, place lid on pot and simmer for 2 hours. Once soup is done simmering, carefully remove chicken. Separate chicken meat from bones and skin. Dice chicken into small pieces. Return chicken to soup and discard bones and skin. In a separate pan, blanch escarole in boiling water for five minutes. Remove escarole from blanching water, drain and chop into bit sized pieces. Add chopped escarole to soup.

Note:

It is important to remove any feathers and rib bones from the chicken prior to cooking.

Variations:

At the same time the escarole is added, try adding 2 cups cooked soup-pasta for a heartier soup. In addition, grated Romano cheese adds a rich flavor. If you are looking to reduce fat, allow the soup to cool before serving. Once the chicken fat condenses on the surface of the soup, skim it off with a spoon and discard. Reheat prior to serving.

Fat-free Cream of Tomato Soup

My mom loves her soups to be scalding hot, if not, she will not eat it. In an attempt to find an alternative to adding cream to a soup, I discovered that the following technique not only yields a fat-free 'creamy' soup, but the use of rice allows the soup to achieve and maintain a very hot temperature. Some of my earliest memories are of my mom and me eating grilled cheese sandwich and tomato soup after my morning pre-school class. I could not think of a better soup to demonstrate this technique on.

Ingredients:

2 cups tomato soup
(or any other homogenous soup)

1 cup pre-cooked white rice
(see Perfect Rice recipe)

Directions:

Heat soup and add cooked rice until it almost begins to boil. Use a submersion blender to 'cream' the rice into the soup for 30 seconds. There will still be individual rice grains, however, most of the rice will have been broken down to thicken and 'cream' the soup.

Note:

If the soup becomes too thick, add some fat free milk until desired consistency is achieved. Bring back to a boil and serve.

Variations:

Another fat-free soup? I know, but rather than adding butter, cream or cheese, try this technique to 'cream' your favorite soups. For a stew-like thickness, refrigerate overnight. Add fat free milk to thin out and heat before serving.

Squash Soup

When I was growing up, my siblings and I would never eat any squash that my mom would cook, except my brother Pat. My father's attempt to get us to eat it was to say 'it tastes just like candy'. Although my mom did add brown sugar to her squash, we did not bite. However, years later it got me thinking, that perhaps a sweeter, rather than a savory flavoring, was the best way to prepare this in a soup. As with most of my soups, the addition of nutmeg is essential.

Ingredients:

1 medium apple—pealed, cored and diced
1 carrot—pealed and chopped
1 stalk celery—chopped
Salt and pepper to taste
¼ cup brown sugar
1 small onion—diced
1 tbl. peanut oil
1 butternut squash—seeded
48 ounces chicken stock
1 tsp. nutmeg

Directions:

Preheat oven to 400°. Cut squash lengthwise and place on a cooking sheet, cut side up. Season with salt and pepper. Divide the brown sugar and place inside seed pocket. Wrap squash in aluminum foil and bake 45 minutes to an hour or until squash is tender when tested with a fork.

In a sauce pan, sauté apple, carrot, celery, onion and oil until tender. Add chicken stock, cover pot with a lid and lower heat to a slow simmer. Remove squash from oven and scoop out squash from the outer peal. Add squash pulp and nutmeg to simmering stock. Using a submersion blender, puree until smooth. Taste soup, additional salt, pepper and brown sugar may be needed.

Note:

Be aware that hot liquids expand rapidly when blended. If using a blender be sure to fill only half way at a time.

Variations:

If you desire a thicker and creamier soup, add 1 cup whole milk or cream and 1 tbl. corn starch and allow to simmer until desired thickness is achieved. You can also use pumpkin or egg corn squash.

Taco Soup

Over the years, I have had my share of 'mishaps' when creating a new recipe. However, throwing out perfectly good food with a less than desired flavor was simply wasteful. So, I learned long ago, that any mistake can be 'disguised' simply by adding taco seasoning—needless to say; I have developed a fondness for this seasoning. This recipe was not a mistake, but rather a variation on my all-time favorite, tomato soup.

Ingredients:

10 oz. condensed tomato soup
10 oz. skim milk
1 cup black beans—canned or reconstituted
1 cup baked tortilla chips—broken up
1 tbl. chopped onion
½ cup mixed greens—chopped
1 cup salsa sauce (see recipe)
½ cup guacamole (see recipe)
1 tsp. taco seasoning

Directions:

Combine condensed soup, milk, beans, salsa, and taco seasoning in a sauce pan and whisk until blended. Bring to a simmer. In a large bowl, toss tortilla chips and mixed greens. Once soup comes to a boil, pour it over the tortilla chips and mixed greens. Top with diced onion and guacamole.

Note:

Be sure not to pour the soup over the chips and mixed greens until just before serving, otherwise the chips and greens will become too soft. Once all ingredients are combined, this must be eaten—it will not store and reheat with a favorable texture.

Variations:

This soup is a great way to use up leftovers. If you have some grilled chicken or other vegetables left from a prior meal, add them to the soup mixture. However, additional taco seasoning may be needed to compensate for the additional ingredients.

Winter Stew

This recipe is my pride and joy. It makes a rich gravy and improves with age if allow to set in the refrigerator for a day. If you are looking for a healthy comfort food, this stew is a must.

Ingredients:

¼ cup olive oil
10 ounces fresh mushrooms—halved and sliced
1 medium onion—chopped
2 cups zucchini—chopped
3 broccoli stalks—pealed and chopped
1 can white beans—with juice
1 can garbanzo beans—with juice
3 tbl. pesto paste (see recipe)
2 tomatoes—skin removed
2 tbl. butter
3 quarts water
1 cup 'soup' pasta—uncooked
Salt and pepper to taste
3 cloves garlic—crushed
½ cup grated parmigian cheese
3 chicken bouillon cubes

Directions:

Boil 3 quarts water and blanch tomatoes. Once skins crack, remove and place under cold water (reserve hot water). Peal off skin and set aside. In a separate sauce pan, sauté mushrooms and onions in oil until soft. Add zucchini, broccoli and bouillon cubes. Add tomatoes and enough of the water they were blanched in to the sautéed vegetables, so all vegetables are covered by two inches of water. Bring to a boil. Add garlic, pesto, butter, white beans, salt and pepper. Simmer for 10 minutes until vegetables are soft and white beans begin to break down. Add garbanzo beans and pasta. Add additional water if stew is too thick to simmer without burning. Allow to simmer for 10 minutes or until pasta is cooked. Stir often to prevent sticking. Remove from heat and stir in cheese. Serve immediately or store in airtight container in refrigerator.

Note:

Be sure not to add the garbanzo beans until after the pasta is cooked. The goal is to cook down the white beans, but to leave the garbanzo beans whole.

Variations:

I recommend serving with stew in a soup bowl with a big piece of garlic bread.

DESSERTS

Apple Cake

My sister-in-law Debbie and I have had a running joke with respect to our adventures in cake baking or as we fondly refer to it as 'a cake from hell'. I came to realize that most of my 'hell-cakes' were a result of boxed cake mixes. This recipe is one of the first alternatives to my inability to achieve success with boxed cake mixes.

Ingredients:

2 eggs
1 cup granulated sugar
1 ½ cup all purpose flour
2 tsp. baking powder
2 tsp. vanilla extract
1 stick butter—chilled
3 apples—pealed, cored and diced

Directions:

Combine flour and baking powder. Cut in butter and set aside. Mix eggs and sugar with electric mixer until smooth. Fold in vanilla and apples to egg mixture. Add flour mixture to egg mixture and mix well. Bake in an 8 inch non-stick pan at 375° for 40-45 minutes.

Note:

Serve with your favorite ice-cream, hot Chocolate Sauce (see recipe) or a Fruit Sauce (see recipe)

Variations:

This recipe has gotten a lot of mileage in my kitchen. Other variations you may try include adding cinnamon to the above recipe or substitute apples for other (non-citrus) fruits. However, be aware of the additional water other fruits may release. An additional ¼ cup of flour may be needed.

Banana Orange Smoothie

This refreshing drink is a great way to help get your daily quota of fresh fruit and tastes like creamsicle ice-cream with less fat.

Ingredients:

1 cup orange juice
¼ apple—with peal but cored
1 banana
3 ice cubes
1 cup frozen vanilla yogurt

Directions:

Place orange juice, apple, banana and ice cubes in a blender. Blend until ice is crushed. Add frozen yogurt and blend for 10 seconds.

Note:

You can omit the ice cubes, but I find that they keep the smoothie cold as well as homogenize the drink—without the ice cubes the fruit tends to separate from the liquid after about five minutes.

Variations:

Be creative. I suggest keeping the orange juice and banana—as they add flavor and thickness, respectively. However, I have used just about every fruit out there. Substitute ½ cup fruit for the apples, such as strawberries, mango, pineapple, or peaches or simply use ½ cup of mixed fruit salad.

Fudge Brownies

When it came to creating a brownie recipe, I was motivated by the same inspiration behind my Flourless Chocolate Cake and Hot Fudge recipes (see recipes). That was, to be able to make Brownies using chocolate chips, rather than running out for some specialized bitter sweet Swiss chocolate.

Ingredients:

6 oz. semi-sweet chocolate chips
4 oz. butter
1 tbl. vanilla extract
2 eggs
½ cup light brown sugar
¼ cup + 1 tbl. flour
½ tsp. baking powder
Pinch of salt

Directions:

Preheat oven to 375º. Spray an 8x8x2 baking pan with cooking spray and cover bottom and sides with wax paper. Spray baking pan a second time, once covered with wax paper. Over a double boiler, melt chocolate chips, butter and vanilla. In a clean stainless steal mixing bowl, combine eggs and sugar and beat well. In a separate mixing bowl, sift together the flour, baking powder and salt. Once chocolate mixture is melted, stir a few spoonfuls into the egg mixture to temper. Add remaining chocolate to egg mixture. Once chocolate and egg mixtures are combined, fold in flour mixture just until blended. Do not over mix. Pour into baking pan and bake for 35 minutes. Remove from oven and allow to cool completely. Lift out of pan and slice.

Note:

Be sure to give the eggs a good beating. Beating the eggs well is what causes that flaky top layer on brownies.

Variations:

I prefer to keep my brownies simply; however, on occasion I will toss in one cup chopped walnuts or mini white chocolate chips.

Chocolate Pasta

If you are a pasta and chocolate lover, you need to give this recipe a try. It is a unique dessert that will be a hit at your next dinner party.

Ingredients:

½ cup flour
¼ cup powdered sugar
1/8 tsp. baking powder
1 tbl. baker's coca powder
1 egg
1 tsp. honey
½ banana
Pinch salt
¼ cup Raspberry Fruit Sauce (see recipe)

Directions:

Sift flour, sugar, baking powder, coca and salt. On a clean surface, make a well in the center of the sifted ingredients. Place the egg in the center of the well and begin to mix in with a fork. Once flour mixture and egg combined use your hands to kneed dough until all dry ingredients are incorporated into the dough. Kneed for five minutes. Additional flour may be required if dough begins to stick. Wrap dough in plastic wrap and allow to set 10 minutes. Divide into quarters and roll out using a pasta roller. Use the linguine attachment to cut into strands. Hang over a wooden dowel to air dry 10 minutes. Place into salted boiling water and cook one to three minutes. Be sure not to over cook. When pasta is cooked, remove from heat. In a separate bowl, add sliced banana and honey. Drain pasta and add to banana and honey. Toss lightly and serve on a platter that has been covered with the fruit sauce.

Note:

If you do not have a pasta roller, you can roll the pasta by hand using a rolling pin.

Variations:

I actually enjoy this pasta best when just tossed with fresh fruit and honey. However, there are as many toppings for Chocolate Pasta as there are for ice-cream. You may want to add a drop of orange extract to the dough while combining with the egg for an exotic flavor.

Creamsicle Ice Cream

Growing up, Creamsicles were one of my favorite flavors of ice cream. Although I still love the taste, I have not found a low fat or yogurt Creamsicle on the market. If you like Creamsicles, try this recipe and you will be amazed how much is tastes like the real thing.

Ingredients:

1 cup frozen yogurt—vanilla
1/3 cup soy milk—plain
2 tbl. orange juice concentrate

Directions:

Place yogurt, milk and 1 tablespoon orange juice concentrate in a blander and combine until smooth. Pore into a plastic container and stir in addition tablespoon of orange juice concentrate. Do not over mix so you can still see orange stripes. Return to freezer for one hour. Serve.

Note:

Allow orange concentrate to thaw slightly, but not to the liquid stage. This will make it easier to stir into the blended yogurt. If you do not mind soft frozen yogurt, serve as soon as you stir in the final tablespoon of orange juice concentrate.

Variations:

As I have mentioned in other recipes, my father got me hooked on banana-orange jell-O. For a unique flavor, toss a banana into the blender.

If you are in the mood to give yourself a treat, you can substitute the yogurt and soy milk for ice cream and milk, respectively.

Flourless Chocolate Cake

During Passover one year, a Jewish friend indicated she was in need of a dessert that had no flour in it. I said I would work on it and by 1am the next morning, I was eating the result of the recipe that follows.

Ingredients:

7 oz. semi-sweet chocolate chips
1 ¾ sticks butter
5 eggs-separated
2 tbl. vanilla extract
¾ cup granulated sugar
Pinch salt
2 tbl. Baker's cocoa powder
1 tsp. cinnamon

Directions:

Preheat oven to 350°. Grease a 10 inch spring-form pan. In a double boiler, melt chocolate and butter until smooth. Remove from heat. In a separate bowl, wisk egg yolks. Temper egg yolks with a little of the melted chocolate mixture. Whisk in egg yolks and vanilla into chocolate mixture. Stir in sugar, salt, cinnamon and cocoa. In a separate bow, whisk egg whites until peaks form (like a meringue). Fold egg whites into chocolate mixture a little at a time. Pour into spring-form pan. Cook on lower rack of oven for 45 minutes or until center tests clean with a cake tester or tooth pick. Remove from oven and open spring-form collar, but keep the collar around the cake. Using the back of a large wooden spoon, press down on top of cake to push air out of it. Remove spring-form collar and allow cake to cool.

Note:

This cake is pretty much a soufflé, so be sure not to over mix while incorporating egg whites.

Variations:

A few variations I have tried include using 1 tbl. vanilla and 1 tbl. orange extracts. This cake is the perfect dessert to serve with a raspberry Fruit Sauce (see recipe).

Instant Spumoni

Walk into any authentic Italian restaurant in New York City and you will find some variation of Spumoni. Typically served as molded ice cream covered with sliced almonds and filled with diced dried fruits, the traditional version is quite an undertaking to make. I decided to leave the traditional version to the restaurants and created this simple recipe. You will get the same result, but with a fresher taste.

Ingredients:

1 red plumb—ripened	¼ cup slivered almonds
2 scoops frozen yogurt—vanilla	Fruit Sauce-frozen (see recipe)

Directions:

Cut plumb in half and remove pit. Using a melon ball scoop, scoop out half of the fruit from each plumb half. This should make a walnut sized whole in each half of the plumb. Cover the plumbs in plastic wrap and freeze for at least one hour. Once frozen, place one scoop of frozen yogurt in the center of each plumb half, cut side up. Place on a plate covered with frozen fruit sauce and sprinkle with slivered almonds. Serve immediately or return to freezer until ready to eat.

Note:

Be sure not to scoop out too much of the plumb center. I like to use frozen strawberries or raspberries to make the fruit sauce for this recipe.

Variations:

This works well with peaches, pears, pineapple rings, or even kiwis that have been pealed. You can use ice cream in place of the yogurt.

Orange-Banana Whip

Long before juice manufactures started to put banana into orange juice, my father had always requested I put bananas in orange jell-o. This recipe is an adaptation to my father's old favorite.

Ingredients:

3 ounces orange jell-o mix	1 ¼ cup orange juice
1 banana—mashed	Ice cubes

Directions:

Follow the directions for 'speed-set' on the jell-o box. However, use hot orange juice in place of hot water. Once you have incorporated the cold juice/ice cubes and ice cubes are melted, whisk in the banana. Refrigerate for 1-2 hours. Remove and whisk again before serving.

Note:

Since bananas spoil quickly once exposed to the air, it is recommended that you eat this within 24 hours.

Variations:

If you are looking for an even lighter whip—after refrigeration, add one cup of whipped cream while whisking before serving.

Quick Apple Crisp

Ever have last minute dinner guests or unexpected visitors stop by for coffee? Well, if you are like me (or my mom)—not serving dessert is simply not an option. This fast, simple and tasty treat has gotten me by in a pinch many times. You can make this while washing the dinner dishes without your guests even noticing.

Ingredients:

½ cup apple—pealed, cored and diced
1 tsp honey
1 tbl. cinnamon graham cracker—crushed
¼ tsp. corn starch
½ tbl. butter
Pinch of cinnamon

Directions:

Combine all ingredients (except graham cracker) and place in a 4 ounce ramekin. Top with graham cracker. Microwave at full power for two minutes. Serve warm or at room temperature. Top with a scoop of vanilla frozen yogurt.

Note:

This recipe is for an individual serving. Increase ingredients one fold for the number of people you need to serve.

Variations:

You can pretty much use whatever fruit you have on hand—except citrus. This works well with pears, peaches, mangos, etc.

Quick Rice Pudding

I simply love rice pudding, but do not like having to spend a few hours to prepare and bake it. I believe this recipe solves that problem, as well as eliminates the eggs that are typically required.

Ingredients:

3/4 cup cooked white rice-cold (see Perfect Rice recipe)
1 ½ cup coconut milk (12 oz.)
¼ golden raisins
2 tsp. vanilla extract
Dash ground nutmeg
½ tsp. ground cinnamon
¼ cup sugar
Pinch salt

Directions:

Combine all ingredients, except rice. Whisk over medium heat until sugar is dissolved and spices are blended. Add in rice and stir over med-high heat for 5 minutes, stirring constantly. Cook until liquid begins to thicken and is creamy. Do not overcook. Remove from heat. Transfer to an air tight container and cover surface with plastic wrap. Allow to come to room temperature and serve. Refrigerate unused portion.

Note:

You can serve this cold, at room temperature or hot. After refrigeration, pudding may become very thick. Simply stir in a little fat free milk until creamy. Top with additional cinnamon, if desired.

Variations:

During the summer, if I am looking for a lighter dessert, I will make Bread Pudding. Simply use 2 cups of diced Italian bread in place of the rice. In addition, I increase the amount of raisins to ½ cup. Once the coconut milk mixture is cooked, add the bread and stir for a minute. There is no need to cook the bread for five minutes.

Rocky-Road Rice Krispies Treats

Once, as I began to make the traditional Rice Krispies Treats and was planning to toss in some chocolate chips, I paused and wondered what would happen if I melted the chocolate with peanut butter but left the marshmallows whole. I believe the balance between the chocolate and peanut butter is the key to this recipe.

Ingredients:

1 cup chocolate chips
½ cup crunchy peanut butter
1 tbl. butter
Pinch of salt
3 cups Rice Krispies cereal
1 cup marshmallows-chopped

Directions:

Combine cereal and marshmallows in a large mixing bowl and set aside. Spray a 9x9x2 pan with cooking spray and set aside. In a sauce pan, combine chocolate chips, peanut butter, butter and salt. Stir over low heat until melted and well mixed. Combine melted chocolate mixture with cereal and marshmallows. Stir until well coated. Press mixture into pan and chill. Cut into bars and serve.

Note:

Unlike traditional Rice Krispies Treats, you do not need to rush once you begin to combine the cereal with the melted chocolate, as it will take longer to set up.

Variations:

In general, Rice Krispies Treats have an unlimited number of possibilities. Whether making them the traditional way, with melted marshmallow or following this recipe, add whatever you desire. In the past, I have made the traditional treats with dried fruits, such as cranberries or diced apricots.

About the Author

Having come from a traditional Italian background, Anthony Michael Vitalone was always surrounded by homemade meals. Being a second generation Italian now living in New York City, "I believe it is essential to maintain the cooking traditions of our ethnic backgrounds. I derive much pride and identity from the simple act of making fresh pasta on a wooden board, in the same way my Grandmothers did."

Traditional Italian cooking is not the only style of food Anthony focuses on. "Variety is the spice of cooking," comments Anthony. He believes that each recipe should have a variety of ingredients, which creates depth of flavor and therefore reduces the amount of butter, salt and oil needed to enhance the flavor of one or two ingredients. In the same sense, Anthony focuses on various ethnic cooking styles, including Greek, Mexican and Chinese. Not only adding variety to a single recipe, but adding variety to the types of meals he prepares.

Anthony is a self taught chef. He estimates that he has watched over 3,000 hours of cooking instruction, has read countless cookbooks and has spent well over 15,000 hours in the kitchen. "I plan to attend formal cooking school someday; however, I wanted to write a cookbook first, with an open mind, from the perspective of an everyday cook."

Index

0-595-24754-7

Printed in the United States
1113800005BA/144